THE MUSICARTA

MODES WORKBOOK

Published by Musicarta Publications, Cape Town, South Africa.

ISBN: 978-0-620-61779-6

Musicarta Modes Workbook
Introduction

Musical modes are scales with a different order of whole-tone and semi-tone steps to those found in the modern Western major scale, which makes music based on them sound different and interesting.

The familiar Western major scale is actually one of the modes – the one which over time has 'won out' because the chords made from it offer the richest and most satisfying harmony to the modern ear.

Three of the other modes – the Mixolydian, Aeolian and Dorian – generate chord families which are still much used in popular music. These modal chord families offer songwriter-composers an interesting alternative to conventional modern harmony and good opportunities for improvising and are form the subject matter of this workbook.

The Musicarta Modes Workbook does not attempt to give a complete historical or academic account of modes. Its purpose is to explain and teach what is useful in modes to the modern popular keyboard player/songwriter/composer, to acquaint the listener's musical ear with the uniquely modal sounds and to present plenty of modal chord sequences for practice and enjoyment.

The workbook is divided into reference, modules and supplements. The reference sections could have been put at the back of the workbook as a collection of appendices – and can indeed be skipped – but they have been left at the front to hopefully encourage readers at some stage to attempt to master the theory of modal harmony.

The second part of the workbook comprises the modules, which methodically build the user's modal 'chord vocabulary' and understanding. Module content and ordering is laid out in the table of contents which follows. The supplements offer master modes chords tables and diversion in the form of the *Spanish Sketches*, cut from the main body of the workbook on the grounds of its harmony not being purely modal.

As well as being a thorough introduction to modes for the modern keyboard player/composer, the Musicarta Modes Workbook is also a practical workbook for learning and improving popular-styles keyboard techniques. Many attractive, syncopated, modern keyboard textures are methodically explained and taught. The MIDI files in the optional extra download, played on the MidiPiano virtual keyboard application (or similar), become teaching videos for every music example in the workbook.

Modes – with the Musicarta Modes Workbook – form an attractive and fruitful focus for both enjoyable musical exploration and sound music-theory progress.

Audio and MIDI download files

NOTE: This is the print-only version of the full Musicarta Publications digital download. If you would like to purchase the audio and MIDI files that accompany this workbook, you can do so from www.musicarta.com – click through on the Sales tab on the navbar. Audio files are mp3 format.

A box like this below a musical example in the workbook gives the reference number of the relevant audio and MIDI example files in the download.

aeo_01_01

If there is no MIDI file for the particular example, the box will state:

(ref.no) (audio only)

Musicarta Modes Workbook
Table of Contents

THE MODES AS SCALES

As scales, modes have a different order of whole tone and semi-tone steps to those found in our regular modern major scale, which makes them sound different and interesting.

Actually, it is more true to say that the modes are made from the modern major scale tones, in their proper order, but starting and finishing on a different note. Modal scales are the major scale we know, but with another note as the tonic (home note). As a result, all the modes can all be found using the white piano keys only – the C major scale tones. The Dorian mode, for example, can be played using the white piano keys from D to D.

Here is a table of all seven modes showing the piano keys that produce them, and a keyboard diagram showing the same information.

Name of mode	White keys	How to say it
Ionian	C to C	Eye-**owe**-nian
Dorian	D to D	**Door**-rian
Phrygian	E to E	Fridge-ian
Lydian	F to F	**Lid**-ian
Mixolydian	G to G	Mix-owe-**lid**-ian
Aeolian	A to A	Eye-**owe**-lian
Locrian	B to B	**Lock**-rian

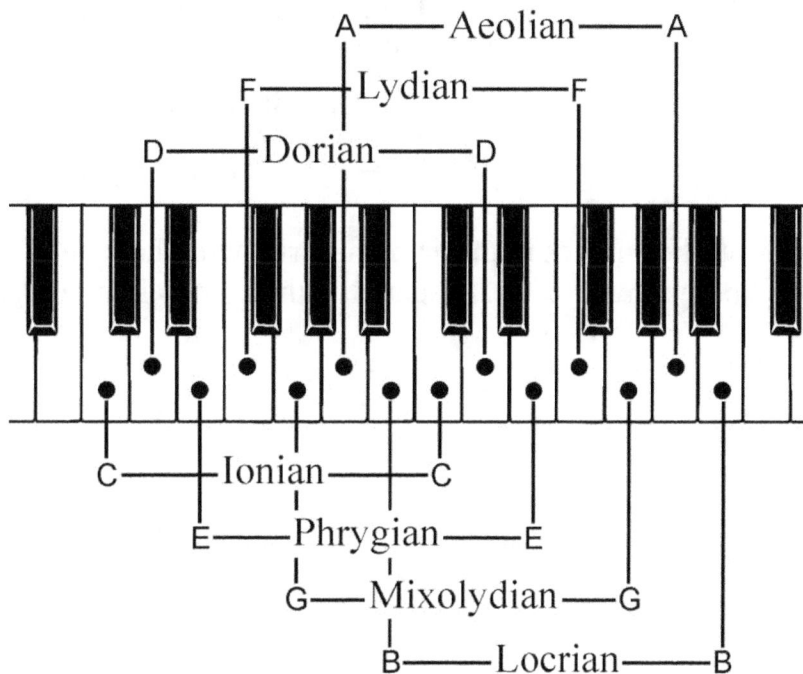

The modes as steps

The important thing about any scale (including the modes) is the pattern of whole tone and semi-tone steps between the scale degrees (the notes of the scale).

Although every white piano key is the same distance from its neighbour, the notes that neighbouring keys make are not all the same distance apart.

Where **there is** a black key between them (at the back of the keyboard), the notes they produce are a whole tone apart.

Where there is **no black key** between them – between B and C, and E and F – the notes they produce are only a semi-tone apart.

Here is the previous diagram showing the whole tone (W) and semi-tone (S) steps between the next-door white keys.

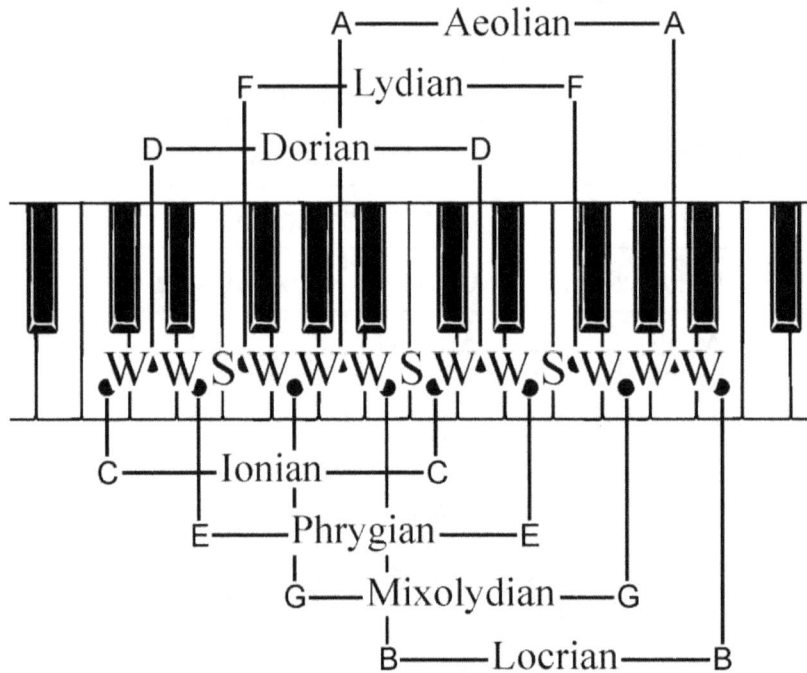

Here are the seven white-key modes in music manuscript with the letters W (for whole tone) and S (for semi-tone) between the notes. Essentially, the modes <u>are</u> these gaps between the tones.

IONIAN – C to C

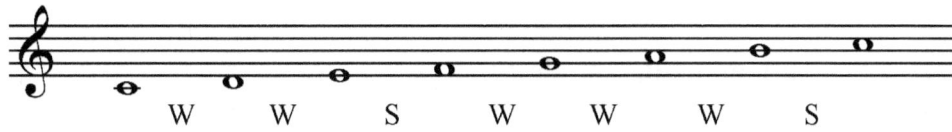

W   W   S   W   W   W   S

DORIAN – D to D

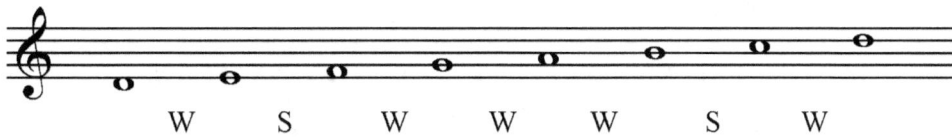

W   S   W   W   W   S   W

PHRYGIAN – E to E

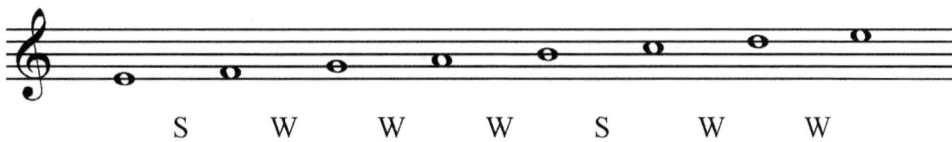

S   W   W   W   S   W   W

LYDIAN – F to F

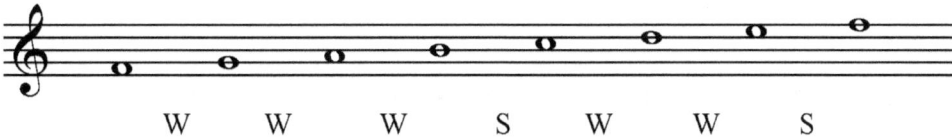

W   W   W   S   W   W   S

MIXOLYDIAN – G to G

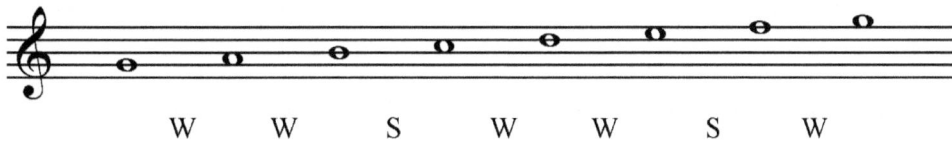

W   W   S   W   W   S   W

AEOLIAN – A to A

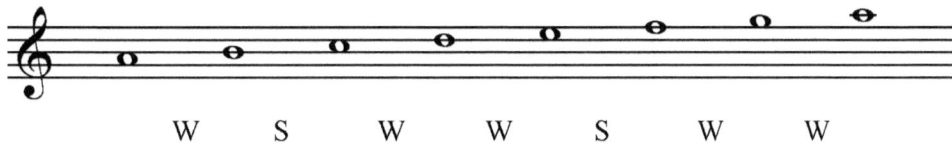

W   S   W   W   S   W   W

LOCRIAN – B to B

S   W   W   S   W   W   W

7

Without the music, the whole-tone/semi-tone patterns of the modes are as follows.

Name of mode	Found using white keys only	Pattern of steps (read ascending from left to right) ● = mode tone (note) W = whole tone step S = semi-tone step
Ionian	C to C	$●W●W●S●W●W●W●S●$
Dorian	D to D	$●W●S●W●W●W●S●W●$
Phrygian	E to E	$●S●W$W●$W●$S●$W●$W●$
Lydian	F to F	$●W●$W●$W●$S●$W●$W●$S●$
Mixolydian	G to G	●$W●$W●$S●$W●$W●$S●$W●$
Aeolian	A to A	●$W●$S●$W●$W●$S●$W●$W●$
Locrian	B to B	●$S●$W●$W●$S●$W●$W●$W●$

You can read off these whole tone/semi-tone distances from the marked-up keyboard diagrams above.

Transposing the modes

If you play these seven modes one after another using only the white piano keys, our modern musical ear hears someone playing a scale of C major starting on different notes (which in fact is exactly what is happening).

To hear the true character of the modes you have to transpose them all to the same starting note. That is, build all seven modes on the same starting note, using the whole tone/semi-tone step patterns.

You can do this using the table above, providing you know how to form whole tone and semi-tone steps on your instrument. Here are the seven modes built on C, in manuscript.

Notice that you now have to state the name of the tonic (home note): C Ionian, C Dorian, C Phrygian, etc.

C IONIAN   (= C major scale from C to C)   Regular major scale

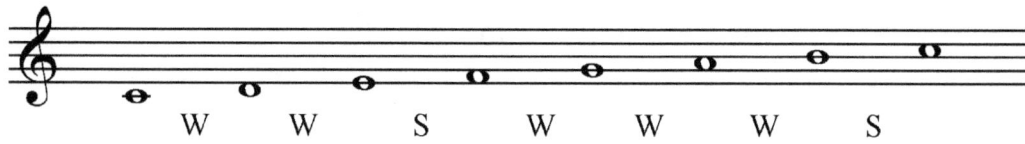

W   W   S   W   W   W   S

C DORIAN   (= B♭ major scale from C to C)   Minor seventh scale

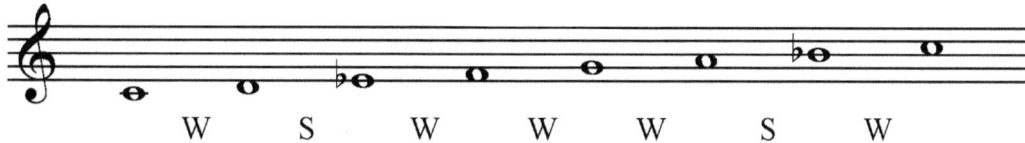

W   S   W   W   W   S   W

C PHRYGIAN   (= Ab major scale from C to C)

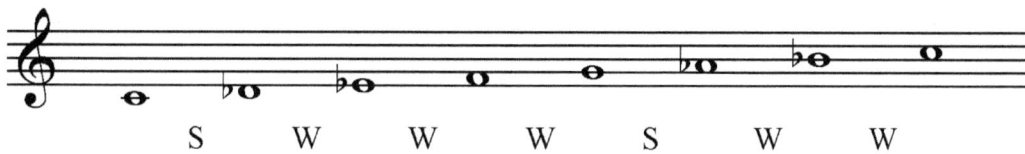

S   W   W   W   S   W   W

C LYDIAN   (= G major scale from C to C)

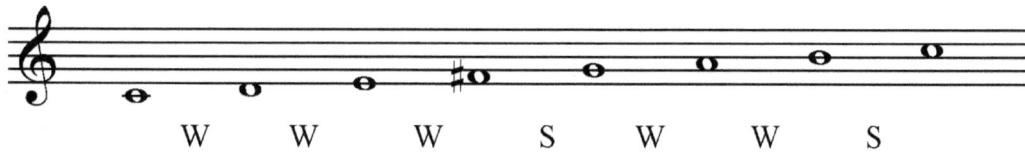

W   W   W   S   W   W   S

C MIXOLYDIAN   (= F major scale from C to C)   Dominant scale

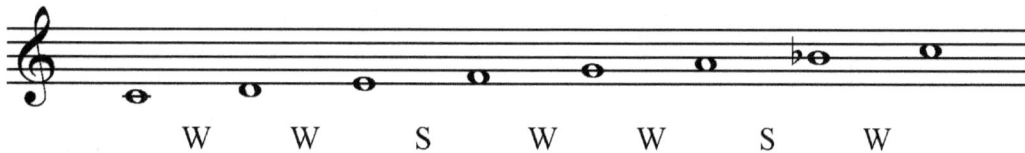

W   W   S   W   W   S   W

C AEOLIAN   (= Eb major scale from C to C)   'Natural minor scale'

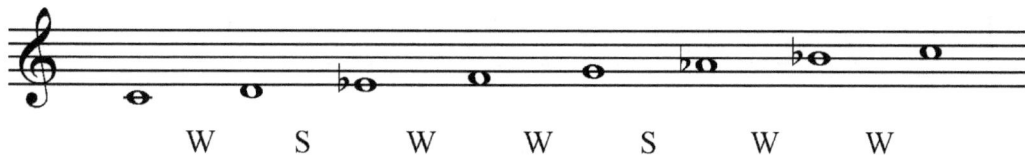

W   S   W   W   S   W   W

C LOCRIAN   (= Db major scale from C to C)

S   W   W   S   W   W   W

9

Building modes using key signatures

Notice in the table above the references like (= F major scale from C to C). You can use key signatures in this way to tell you which of the semi-tones in the octave to use to create your chosen mode.

For example, to play Dorian mode from D, you use just the white keys – the C major scale tones, in fact. C major is a whole tone below D. Using this rule, you can play the Dorian mode from G using the scale tones of F major.

Likewise, if the scale tones of C major – the white piano keys – from F to F give the Lydian mode (and C is a fifth above F), then the Lydian mode on A will use the key signature of E major.

Here is a table which shows this information – for the white keys only.

Starting note ▽	Mode required							Key signature to use
	Ionian (C to C)	Dorian (D to D)	Phrygian (E to E)	Lydian (F to F)	Mixolydian (G to G)	Aeolian (A to A)	Locrian (B to B)	
C	C	B♭	A♭	G	F	E♭	D♭	
D	D	C	B♭	A	G	F	E♭	
E	E	D	C	B	A	G	F	
F	F	E♭	D♭	C	B♭	A♭	G♭	
G	G	F	E	D	C	B♭	A♭	
A	A	G	F	E	D	C	B♭	
B	B	A	G	F♯	E	D	C	
	(Same note)	Whole tone below	Two whole tones below	Perfect fourth below	Perfect fourth above	Minor third above	Semi-tone above	

Here are the key signatures required.

Here are the examples written out for C. Note that the accidentals are still placed in the music itself (in brackets) to show which notes the key signature affects. This would not normally be done.

C Ionian - C major scale tones

W   W   S   W   W   W   S

C Dorian - B♭ major scale tones

W   S   W   W   W   S   W

C Phrygian - A♭ major scale tones

S   W   W   W   S   W   W

C Lydian - G major scale tones

W   W   W   S   W   W   S

C Mixolydian - F major scale tones

W   W   S   W   W   S   W

C Aeolian - E♭ major scale tones

W   S   W   W   S   W   W

C Locrian - D♭ major scale tones

S   W   W   S   W   W   W

How the modes differ from the major scale

Another helpful perspective is to consider how the modes differ from the modern major scale. You have to know your major scales, of course, and remember that in the major scale, the semi-tone steps are between the third and fourth, and seventh and eighth (octave) scale degrees.

Mode	Found using white keys only	Significant difference from major scale
Mixolydian	G to G	The dominant seventh scale – the seventh is lowered a semi-tone (♭7)
Lydian	F to F	The fourth is raised a semitone (♯4)
Aeolian	A to A	The descending melodic minor scale (♭3, ♭6, ♭7). Sometimes called the 'natural minor'.
Dorian	D to D	The minor seventh scale – third and seventh both lowered a semi-tone (♭3 and ♭7). Same as Aeolian except that the sixth is not flattened.

Modes exercise

Building all seven modes on every possible starting note using the whole tone/semi-tone step patterns is not necessary.

The reason is that, for all practical purposes, only three modes (apart from the Ionian mode, our modern major scale) survive – the Mixolydian, Dorian and Aeolian. The other modes are too close to the modern major scale to remain distinct.

(For example, if you play B to B on the white keys – the Locrian mode – the modern ear simply hears the C major scale being played from the seventh degree to the seventh degree.)

You should however be able to build these three modes, not only to use as improvising scales, but in order to find the useful families of chords we explore in the workbook modules.

There is already a table in this module showing all the modes built on C and a table of their whole and semi-tone steps. If you know how to form whole tone and semitone steps reliably on your instrument, you can use this table to play the modes starting on any note.

So, using all the resources given so far, create the following modal scales on the given tonics (home/starting notes).

First set. Only one black key (per scale) needed.

Starting note	Mode	Pattern of steps (ascending)
G	Ionian	$●W●W●S●W●W●W●S●$
C	Mixolydian	●$W●$W●$S●$W●$W●$S●$W●$
E	Aeolian	●$W●$S●$W●$W●$S●$W●$W●$
A	Dorian	$●W●S●W●W●W●S●W●$

Second set. Two black keys required.

Starting note	Mode	Pattern of steps (ascending)
F	Mixolydian	●$W●$W●$S●$W●$W●$S●$W●$
D	Ionian	●$W●$W●$S●$W●$W●$S●$W●$
G	Aeolian	●$W●$S●$W●$W●$S●$W●$W●$
E	Dorian	$●W●S●W●W●W●S●W●$
B	Aeolian	●$W●$S●$W●$W●$S●$W●$W●$

Third set. Three black keys required.

Starting note	Mode	Pattern of steps (ascending)
C	Aeolian	●$W●$S●$W●$W●$S●$W●$W●$
E	Mixolydian	●$W●$W●$S●$W●$W●$S●$W●$
B♭	Mixolydian	●$W●$W●$S●$W●$W●$S●$W●$
F	Dorian	$●W●S●W●W●W●S●W●$
B	Dorian	$●W●S●W●W●W●S●W●$

THE MODES AS KEYS

Only four modes offer anything harmonically useful in the modern popular music context. They are the Ionian, the Mixolydian, the Dorian and the Aeolian.

The Ionian mode

The Ionian mode survives as our modern major scale and key system, and accounts for the greater part of all the music we hear today. Learning to 'pull the levers' of this modern harmonic system should be the first priority of anyone wishing to be a creative modern musician, and teaching this is the aim of the Musicarta Key Chords Vol.1 workbook. Use the Musicarta Chords navbar tab to access other chords study pages. (You do not need to have completed the chord progressions series to study modes.)

The Mixolydian mode

The Mixolydian mode differs from the modern major scale in having a flattened seventh scale degree. The characteristic sound of the Mixolydian mode is therefore chord 'bVII' – 'Flat Seven', a major chord one whole tone below the tonic (I) chord. One result is the chord sequence bVII–IV–I – an iconic rock sound and a great jamming sequence explored in the Mixolydian Two module.

Exploration of the Mixolydian mode starts on page 16.

The Dorian and Aeolian modes

The Dorian and Aeolian are both minor modes – the third scale degree is flattened.

The distinctive feature of the minor modes is that their all-important dominant chord (built on the fifth degree of the scale) is a minor chord.

To the modern ear, a minor dominant chord (v) is not convincing. As a result, the minor modes evolved into the modern minor key with the sharpening of the third to give the major dominant V chord. The modern minor key is therefore not a mode.

The weakness of the minor dominant (v) chord can however be got round, and Aeolian and Dorian chord sequences persist in jazz, funk and New Age music.

Exploration of the minor modes starts in Minor Modes (1) on page 30.

The modes as keys

Note: This section requires a working knowledge of the Roman numeral system (RNS) of naming chords – the 'chords in any key' system used to discuss and think about musical harmony and chords generally. Visit the Musicarta RNS web page (via the site Chords tab) for an introduction. The Roman numeral system is a powerful addition to your musical theory arsenal! (The system will 'sink in' to some degree if you just keep taking note.)

The Mixolydian mode

In order to appreciate the chord families of the modes, we have to compare them with the chords of modern major and minor harmony. We compare the chords of the Mixolydian mode with the modern major key, because they both have a major third degree.

First, revise what you know about the chords of the modern major key.

Modern major key triads (from white keys C to C – the major scale)						
Chords:	I	ii	iii	IV	V	vi	vii°
Quality:	major	minor	minor	major	major	minor	dimin.
Example:	C	Dm	Em	F	G	Am	Bdim

This table tells you that:

- The simplest chord (a root position triad) built on the first degree of the major scale will be major (Roman numeral system I, upper case);
- The chord built on the second degree of the scale will be minor (ii, lower case);

… and so on. It is this mixture of major and minor chords that produces what we hear as 'key' – specifically, the major key of I (here, C major).

Now here is the same analysis of the chords produced by the notes of the Mixolydian mode, here played from G to G (to stay on the white keys).

Mixolydian mode triads (white notes G to G)						
Chords:	I	ii	iii°	IV	v	vi	♭VII
Quality:	major	minor	dimin.	major	minor	minor	major
Example:	G	Am	Bdim	C	Dm	Em	F

Now we compare the two sets of chords. The differences are highlighted.

Modern major (= Ionian)	major	minor	minor	major	major	minor	dimin.
	I	**ii**	**iii**	**IV**	**V**	**vi**	**vii°**
Mixolydian	**I**	**ii**	**iii°**	**IV**	**v**	**vi**	**♭VII**
	major	minor	dimin.	major	minor	minor	major

The significant difference is that the Mixolydian mode has a minor (and therefore weak) dominant (v) chord but a strong (and useful) ♭VII chord. This gives a fruitful pair of chords – I and ♭VII, two major chords a whole tone apart, the upper one the tonic (home) chord.

The exploration of Mixolydian harmony starts on page 16.

The minor modes and the modern minor key

The following music theory is included for teachers and others interested in music theory. We start learning the module riff at the section 'The i and ♭VII (One and Flat Seven) pair' below. Feel free to skip forward if you want to.

Here is a comparison between the chord families of the modern minor key and the Dorian and Aeolian modes.

Modern minor key triads (from the A harmonic minor scale)						
Chords: **i**	**ii°**	**♭III**	**iv**	**V**	**♭VI**	**vii°**
Quality: minor	dimin.	major*	minor	major	major	dimin.

Here is the chord family of the Dorian mode.

Dorian mode triads (white notes D to D)						
Chords: **i**	**ii**	**♭III**	**IV**	**v**	**♭vi°**	**♭VII**
Quality: minor	minor	major	major	minor	dimin.	major

Here are the chords of the Aeolian mode.

Aeolian mode triads (white notes A to A)							
Chords:	**i**	**ii°**	**♭III**	**iv**	**v**	**♭VI**	**♭VII**
Quality:	minor	dimin.	major	minor	minor	major	major

If we strip out the little-used diminished chords and then compare the Aeolian and Dorian chord families with the modern classical minor key, this is what we find.

Modern harmonic minor	minor			major	minor	major	major	
	i			**♭III**	**iv**	**V**	**♭VI**	
Dorian	**i**	**ii**		**♭III**	**IV**	**v**		**♭VII**
	minor	minor		major	major	minor		major
Aeolian	**i**			**♭III**	**iv**	**v**	**♭VI**	**♭VII**
	minor			major	minor	minor	major	major

The significant differences are:

- In both the Aeolian and Dorian modes, the all-important dominant chord is minor (v), compared to the major V chord of the modern minor key.
- Both modes have a ♭VII chord – which often acts as the cadencing chord (♭VII–i) in the place of the missing major V chord.
- The Dorian mode has a major IV (subdominant) chord, whereas the Aeolian mode and the modern minor key both have minor iv chords.

The exploration of minor mode harmony starts in the third module on page 30.

There are comprehensive tables of the essential chords in the Ionian, Mixolydian, Aeolian and Dorian modes in the most useful keys at the back of the book.

THE MIXOLYDIAN MODE (1)

The significant difference between the modern major key and the Mixolydian mode is that the Mixolydian mode has a minor (and therefore weak) dominant (v) chord but a strong (and useful) ♭VII ('Flat Seven') chord. This gives a fruitful pair of chords – I and ♭VII, two major chords a whole tone apart, the upper one being the tonic (home) chord. This module examines that I–♭VII pair's potential.

I and ♭VII in G Mixolydian

As the white piano keys give us G Mixolydian without any alteration, we'll examine the I–♭VII pair in G Mixolydian.

Any three-note chord (triad) can appear in three versions – root position, first inversion and second inversion. This means there are three next-door pairs of I and ♭VII chords.

mix_01_01

Here are the six chords in an analysis table.

G Mixolydian						
Scale deg. (top note)	**R**	**m7**	**5**	**4**	**3**	**2**
Chord	**I**	**♭VII**	**I**	**♭VII**	**I**	**♭VII**
	G	**F**	**G**	**F**	**G**	**F**
Inversion	△	△	○	○	□	□

The circle, square and triangle symbols indicate the inversion used.

Symbol	Inversion	Which is the root (name-note)?
△	First inversion	The top note is the name-note
○	Root position	The bottom note is the name-note
□	Second inversion	The middle note is the name-note

If you do not read music, you can still find the chords using the keyboard diagrams or the Musicarta Visual Glossary – click through and print one for reference.

Play the descending chords at your keyboard. Note that the first inversion pair repeats at the end.

G	F	G	F	G	F	G	F
△	△	○	○	□	□	△	△

mix_01_02

The two chords in each pair (in each bar) are exactly the same shape – all you have to do is move your hand one key to the left. It's better, though, once you have found the chords, to use the fingering given.

Notice that we now have a key signature – G major – and that we have to cancel out the black key F sharp to get the Mixolydian mode. Why bother with the key signature then? To let the musician know that we're 'in G', even if it is a mode.

Riff One

If you add a left hand/bass part simply playing the roots of the chords (notes G and F) and a bit of a swing beat, you can already get a riff like this.

mix_01_03

Before you try copying the audio, break it down. Listen to what the left hand and what the right hand does. Tap out the rhythm away from the keyboard.

1 (2 3) 4 (5) 6 7 8   1 (2 3) 4 (5) 6 7 8

T   T   R R L   T   T   R R L

mix_01_BM1

The beat is counted in quavers, above the beat map. If nothing happens on a particular quaver beat, the number is in brackets.

The letters T, L, R below the beat map stand for together, left, right, and indicate which hand or hands play. Feel free to forget the rhythm temporarily and tap the pattern as slowly as you need, to be sure that the TLR 'events' come in the right order.

Here's the music for the riff.

G   F   G   F   G   F   G   F

mix_01_03

Riff Two: I and ♭VII over a pedal bass

This I–♭VII string of chords is often heard over a pedal bass. A pedal bass is a single bass note played under any number of different chords, and which doesn't change when the chords change. In this case, it is G. 'Pedal' comes from the organ, where the bass notes are played with the feet pushing down big key-shaped pedals.

mix_01_04

Do the rhythmic analysis again.

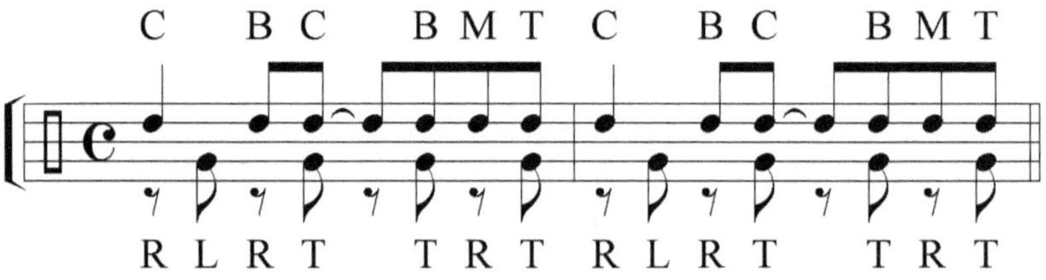

mix_01_BM2

No count is given – something happens on every quaver beat except beat 5.

The left hand plays off the beat all the way through. Slow it right down and use the TLR analysis to make sure you get the TLR 'events' in the right order.

The top row of letters is the 'bottom, middle, top' (BMT) analysis. You fill up quaver slots by playing the bottom, middle and top notes of the chord separately. (C stands for <u>C</u>hord – play the full chord, **or** just the top note.) Listen to the live audio riff as you read the beat map until you can hear how the two things refer to each other, then try to play.

Here is the music for the riff.

Riff Three: I and ♭VII chords in the left hand – with tonic pedal

Here is another tonic pedal construction, with the chords in the left hand.

mix_01_05

Use the circle and triangle symbols to get the chord shapes from the keyboards diagram above if you need to.

Look at the chord symbols – you see 'slash bass' symbols. The slash bass symbols here say "This is an F chord with a different note – G – at the bottom." Slash bass chord symbols can be written with the added bass note either under or after the chord symbol – both ways are shown here.

Ear training exercise

Because you have the chords in the left hand, you can play a 'thinner' right hand – you don't need to play chords in both hands. Here's one possible bottom-middle-top (BMT) broken-chord right hand.

Listen to this audio clip.   mix_01_06

You hear the familiar G and F major broken chords in the right hand, played in a repeated rhythmic pattern.

- Find the chords at the keyboard. You know they will be G, F, G and F chords.
- Work out the right hand broken chord rhythm.
- Listen to the broken chord pattern in terms of bottom, middle, top notes and break up your chords accordingly.

Answers

The beat map (rhythm) is as follows.

Here are the chords with the BMT (bottom, middle, top) analysis shown.

Listen and check the BMT analysis against the audio again.

mix_01_06

Here is the written-out music for this riff.

Riff Four (variation)

Here's another similar riff. The right hand notes come more quickly and are broken up into groups of three, three and two – a common trick in popular music.

mix_01_07

Try to get the performance without the written music if you can.

Here is the MS if required.

The above riffs are mainly for inspiration and practice. You listen to them 'with a thinking ear' – to hear how they're made. Even if you can't play them at first, you will probably discover some playable G Mixolydian riff that's 'a bit like' the example along the way.

Keep your own version and try again. You can expect learning these riffs to take a number of methodical attempts. Enjoy the journey!

THE MIXOLYDIAN MODE (2)

Mixolydian ♭VII–IV–I riffs

The most recognisable Mixolydian chord sequence is ♭VII–IV–I (Flat Seven, Four, One).

Riff One

Find the chords on the right hand side of this keyboards diagram.

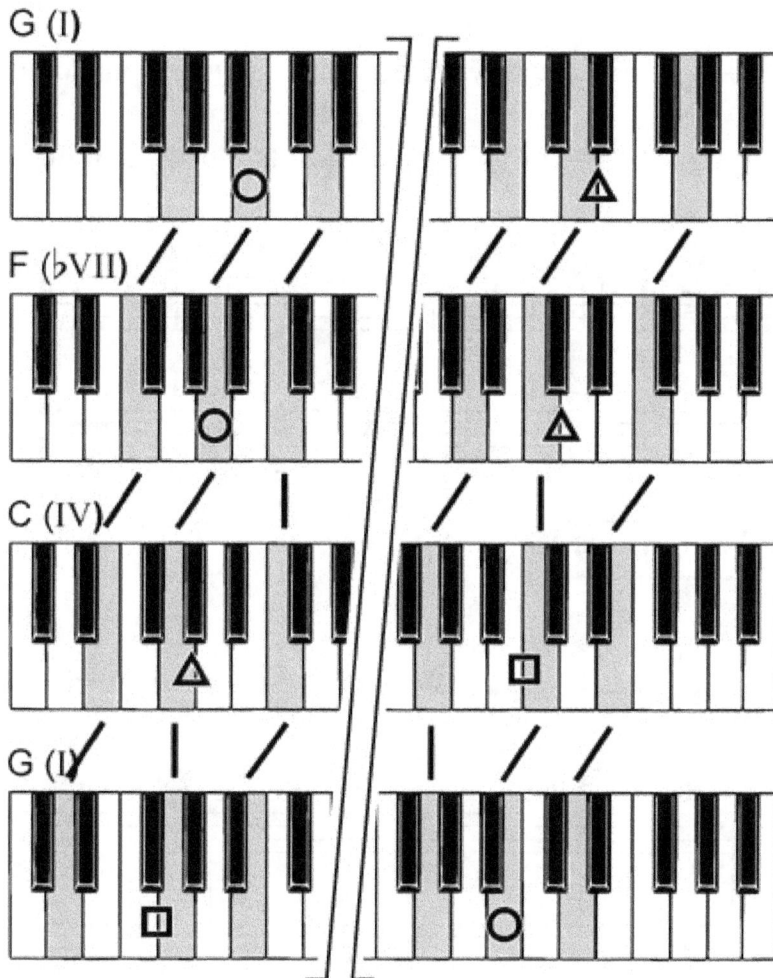

Play the four chords from the top down.

mix_02_01

MIXOLYDIAN TWO

For our classic ♭VII–IV–I riff, we need just the last three chords.

The chords are written an octave higher than they are played, to save you reading lots of ledger lines.

The falling top line (scale tones m7 – 6 – 5) is instantly recognisable. You can play either the roots in the bass, or a G pedal bass.

This combination of chords is the basis of lots of driving rock riffs. Here's an example.

Riff Two

mix_02_04

Here is a less powered-up riff which uses the same chords. In the audio clip you hear a pedal G bass, a root-of-the-chord bass, and a walking bass (which uses a B♭ descending for effect).

The music shows only the basic chords. Pick up the rhythm from the audio clip. Octaves are used in the left hand, rocking bottom-top to add rhythm. Later modules will walk you through building up complicated two-handed syncopation like this.

Riff Three

Here is a riff in rock three-four time using all four chords.

These are the chords.

| G | F | C | G |
| I | ♭VII | IV | I |

Here is the chord sequence.

G	F	C	G
G	F	C	C
G	F	C	G
G	F	C	C

This music is very simplified.

mix_02_05

You will be shown how to play the more rhythmically complicated keyboard textures in later modules.

Riff Four

Now find the chords on the left hand side of the keyboards diagram.

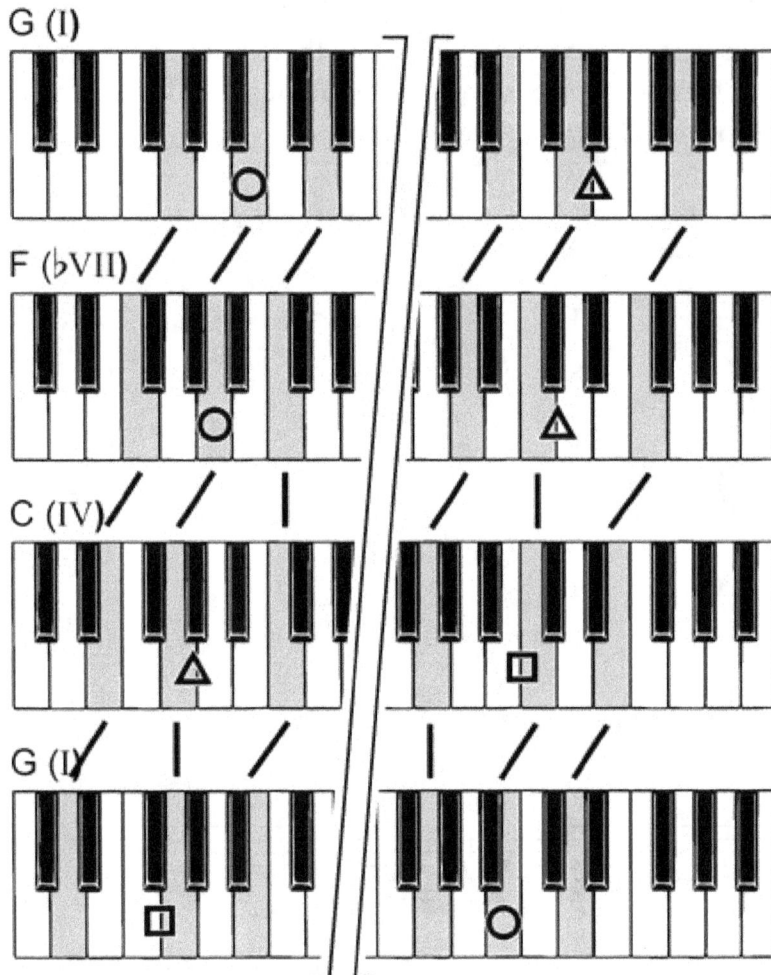

Play them *from the bottom up*. Watch out for the bass clef in the written-out music.

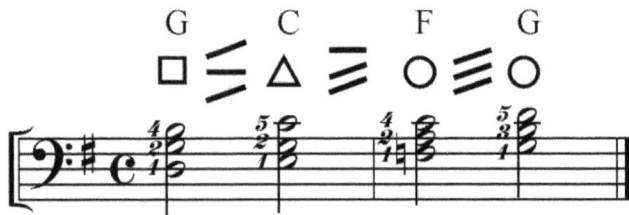

Note how, in all these manuscript examples, the key signature is the classical G major (to indicate that G is still the tonic/home chord. The F natural (♮) throughout indicates the Mixolydian mode.

Here's the riff based on these chords. Learn the chords from the MIDI and play along

mix_02_06

We have changed the inversions and we're playing the chords in the reverse order so that they are rising rather than falling.

Riff Five – a four-chord Mixolydian sequence

Here is a riff which uses the Mixolydian minor dominant (D minor in G Mixolydian).

Find the first four chords in this keyboards diagram.

G (I)

Dm (v)

F (♭VII)

C (IV)

G (I)

Dm (v)

29

mix_02_07

Note that, to avoid leger lines, the chords are written an octave higher than they are played. Play them in an easy groove like this.

mix_02_08

Play it through twice. So far, our chord sequence looks like this:

G   Dm   F   C

G   Dm   F   C

Next, use the bottom four chords from the keyboards diagram (from F down).

mix_02_09

Play them twice and add them onto the first chord sequence.

G	Dm	F	C
G	Dm	F	C
F	C	G	Dm
F	C	G	Dm

Double up phrases to make the whole thing longer. Use the first four chords for your song verse and the second four chords for the chorus.

Notice the restlessness of this Mixolydian chord sequence. You don't quite know where 'home' is. To out modern ear, the modes (except for the Ionian) aren't quite fully formed as a key system – which is precisely why the Ionian 'won out' as the modern major, and the minor modes got a major dominant (V) chord and became the modern classical minor key.

Here's a beat map for the complicated rhythm in the last audio clip.

mix_02_BM1 (audio only)

Mixed major/Mixolydian sequences

There's no hard and fast rule to say we can't mix modal and modern major/minor harmonies. In fact, the ♭VII chord is often 'borrowed in' to regular pop songs.

Find these four chords.

mix_02_10

The only difference to the previous riff is that there is no F natural sign (♮) in the D chord, so the D chord stays major. Notice how the top note falls a semi-tone every chord change – something considered desirable in music generally.

Here's a riff based on the four chords.

mix_02_11

The left hand in this riff uses different inversions of the same chords.

mix_02_12

Use them on their own as a simpler riff left hand if you wish.

Finally, here's the third and final set of possible inversions, and a riff built on them.

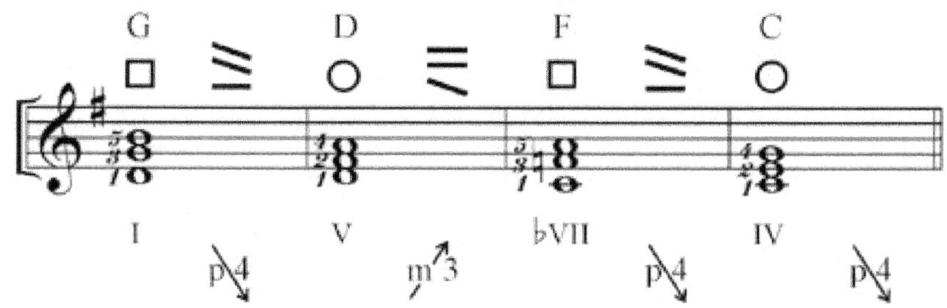

mix_02_13

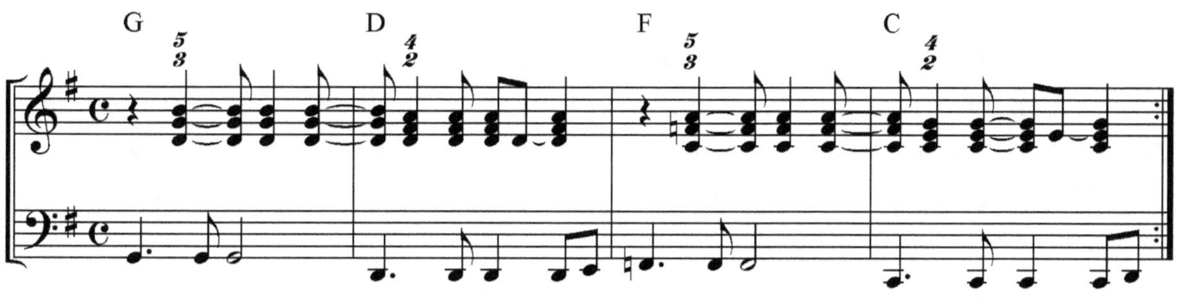

mix_02_14

THE MINOR MODES

This module starts our look at the minor modes. Listen to the module riff you build up to.

min_01_01

The i–♭VII (One, Flat Seven) pair

In both minor modes (Aeolian and Dorian) the all-important 'five' chord (the dominant) is minor, and this is considered weak as a cadencing chord. The major ♭VII chord, which is available in both modal minors, often acts as a substitute.

Both the Aeolian and Dorian modes have this fruitful i-♭VII chord combination (highlighted in the table below) – the minor tonic (home chord) with a major chord a whole tone below.

Just as I and V in regular major keys (and i and V in the minor) can support lots of music on their own, so i and ♭VII in minor modes are a vital and fruitful pair of chords.

Aeolian	minor		major	minor	minor	major	major
	i		**♭III**	**iv**	**v**	**♭VI**	**♭VII**
Dorian	**i**	**ii**	**♭III**	**IV**	**v**		**♭VII**
	minor	minor	major	major	minor		major

The module riff

Listen to the module riff again (top of page).

The riff uses the two pairs of i-♭VII chords that you can find using only white piano keys – A minor and G, and D minor and C.

Find the inversions of the A minor and G chords from the keyboard diagrams below.

At some point, you will want to study the tables you see one these pages. They may look very academic, but they contain a wealth of useful musical information.

A minor and G chords							
Chord	i	♭VII	i	♭VII	i	♭VII	i
	Am	G	Am	G	Am	G	Am
Top note	tonic	m7	5	4	m3	2	tonic
	1st inversion △		root position ◯		2nd inversion ☐		△

The table tells you that six notes in the octave (the six top notes of the three inversions of the two chords) can be harmonised these two chords. In the tables, the 'top notes' are counted from the root of the A minor (home/tonic) chord.

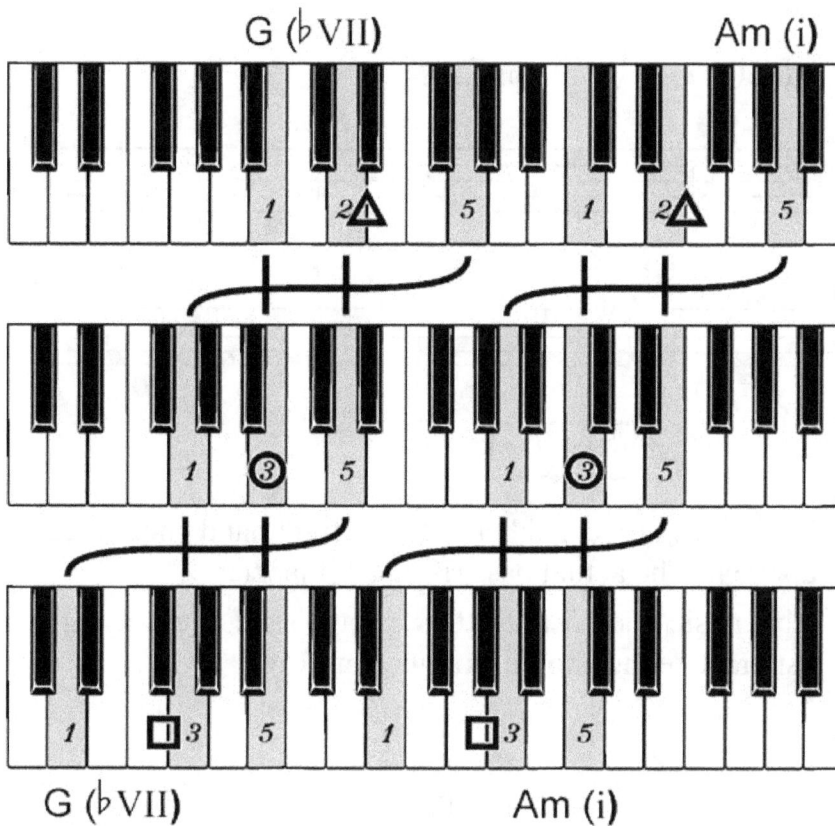

G (♭VII)   Am (i)

Key to the symbols.

Symbol	Inversion	Which is the root (name-note)?
△	First inversion	The top note is the name-note
○	Root position	The bottom note is the name-note
□	Second inversion	The middle note is the name-note

The wavy line in the voice movement line diagrams clearly shows how the top note goes to the bottom (or vice versa) as you flip between inversions. Practice with the fingering in the keyboards diagram, to encourage a good hand position.

The inversions you see in the illustration could be played anywhere on the keyboard. The G chords you will play will be only one key below (to the left of) the A minor chords of the same inversion.

The chords in pairs

Find the descending string of eight alternating A minor and G chords. Use the triangle, circle and square symbols to help (even if you do read music). The pairs of A minor/G chords are the same shape, only one key apart.

The chords are written an octave higher than played, to save a lot of leger lines. To start building the riff, play the chords descending, an octave lower than written (*8vb* – start with the right thumb on middle C).

Am △ G   Am ○ G   Am □ G   Am △ G

min_01_02

The riff has a 'pedal bass' – a bass note A repeated between the right hand chords regardless of what chord is being played above it. The actual bass riff is a bit jazzier.

The riff also has a jazzy beat – the music doesn't show this, for the sake of clarity. Imitate the audio/MIDI performances or just practice the chords straight, for now.

The D minor and C chords

C (♭VII)   Dm (i)

C (♭VII)   Dm (i)   51

Next, find the D minor and C chords. Use the keyboards diagram rather than the music even if you do read, to practice 'seeing the music in the keyboard'. Remember that the keyboards diagram just shows what shape of chord to play, not where to play it.

Practise flipping through the inversions of D minor and C in the same way as before. Browse the table which follows to increase your stock of 'really useful theory'.

D minor and C chords							
Chord	i	♭VII	i	♭VII	i	♭VII	i
	Dm	C	Dm	C	Dm	C	Dm
Top	tonic	m7	5	4	m3	2	tonic
note	1st inversion △		root position ○		2nd inversion □		△

Now learn to play the D minor and C Chords in exactly the same pattern as the A minor and G chords before.

Dm △ C   Dm ○ C   Dm □ C   Dm △ C

min_01_03

The D minor/C part of the riff comes half way through. The music is a bit simplified – it doesn't show the jazzy beat. The music is written where it is played.

The whole riff: AABA form

Listen to the module riff again, paying attention to its 'shape'.

min_01_01

You hear:

- The descending string of eight alternating A minor and G chords twice, then
- The same eight-chord pattern using D minor and C chords, then

37

- The A minor and G string again, then
- An 'outro'/ending.

(An 'outro' is the opposite of an <u>intro</u>-duction!)

Basically, we have one 'thing' (the A minor/G chords) twice, another thing (the D minor/C chords) once, then the first 'thing' again. (The outro is just tacked on.)

If we call the first thing 'A' and the second thing 'B', we have what's called 'AABA form' – two 'A strains' (sections), one 'B strain' then another 'A strain'. You'll find AABA form a lot in music, especially in jazz standard songs. Listen out for it!

Putting it together

Your main aim is to practice efficiently so you achieve you goal as quickly as possible.

- Slow it down until you can play both eight-chord strings. If you can't play one of them:
  - identify which bit is difficult for you and what's going wrong;
  - fix that then integrate the repair back into the string of chords.
- Work on the jump from the A minor/G keyboard position to the D minor/C keyboard position and back (this would usually be a difficulty).

Then – enjoy! The main purpose of a riff like this is either to back a solo, or just to get into the groove and enjoy your own playing. Note that it's fine to play the whole riff slower than the demo audio tracks.

More i-♭VII riffs

You can build up whole riffs, swapping between just i-♭VII chords: Here are two 'play by ear' examples to copy. Use the MIDI clips to see exactly what is going on.

| min_01_04 | min_01_05 |

TRANSPOSING i-♭VII

This module continues our look at the minor modes. Here are the riffs you'll learn to play in this module.

min_02_04	min_02_05	min_02_06

Finding i and ♭VII anywhere

The previous module introduced the two i and ♭VII ('one and flat seven') chord pairs you can find using the white piano keys only – A minor and G, and D minor and C.

But we can't be limited to just the white piano keys. For lots of reasons, we want to be able find i–♭VII pairs in different places on the keyboard.

Transposing a simple pair of chords like this up or down on your keyboard is a core skill. Here are the logical steps of the process.

- i is a minor chord. We know because the RNS (Roman numeral system) chord symbol is lower case, not I (upper case), and lower case is reserved for minor chords. Because it's 'Number One', it's the naming chord of the mode or key: i in A Aeolian minor is the chord A minor; and so on.

- ♭VII is a major chord. We know because the Roman numerals are upper case ('capitals') – not lower case, which would be vii and indicate a minor chord. We number chord according to the major scale, and the seventh degree of the major scale is a semi-tone below the tonic/home note. The flat sign in front of the VII asks for a note one semi-tone lower than that, i.e., a whole tone below i.

- So: i and ♭VII are built on roots a whole tone apart. i is the higher of the two and is a minor chord; ♭VII is lower and is a major chord

Here is a table of sample i–♭VII pairs.
Ideally, you should be able to work out these pairs in your head.

i	♭VII
the (upper) minor chord	the (lower) major chord
All-white-key combinations	
Am	G
Dm	C
One-black-key combinations	
Em	D
Gm	F
Two-black-key combinations	
Cm	B♭
Bm	A

Broken chord patterns and BMT analysis

In modern popular keyboard styles, the right hand mostly plays three-note chords, and you very often break these chords up and play the three chord tones one after the other in a nice rhythmic pattern. That way, you get more 'mileage' out of the chords you've learnt – and fill more bars with great music.

'BMT analysis' is Musicarta's broken chord shorthand. Thinking in terms of bottom, middle and top (BMT) chord tones is a powerful technique. After a while, broken chord patterns become semi-automatic; you set your hands to play a BMT pattern and 'let your fingers do the talking'.

Broken chord patterns also offer more music for less thinking. Instead of thinking about three or four (or more0 notes, you only have to "think" the pattern. Also, you can transpose a pattern more easily – all you need to do is get your hand over the new chord and press the 'play pattern' button in your head.

The i–♭VII broken chord riffs – Number 1

We first explore broken chord patterns in the G minor and F i–♭VII position.

Here are the chords you need in a keyboard diagram.

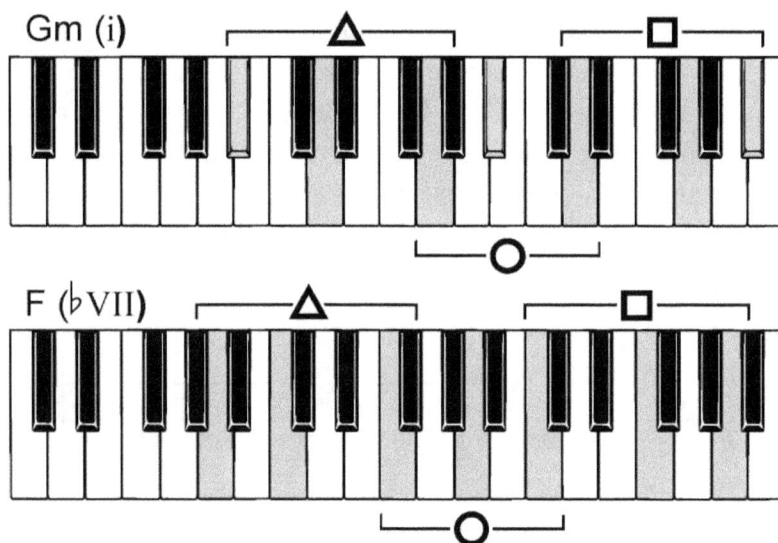

The chord tones are shaded and bracketed according to their inversions. Note that the inversion brackets only show you the **shape** of the chord, not **where** the chord you want actually is. Refer to the key again:

Symbol	Inversion	Shape	Which is the root (name-note)?
△	First inversion	𝄞	The top note is the name-note
○	Root position	𝄞	The bottom note is the name-note
□	Second inversion	𝄞	The middle note is the name-note

Start building the riff.

min_02_01

The first two bars of the music show the actual notes as you hear them in the example audio clip. The next two bars – which sound exactly the same – show the chords you are playing, and how they are broken up into top, middle and bottom notes. You play top, middle, bottom, top (T, M, B, T) for each chord except the last F chord, which only uses top, middle, bottom (T, M, B).

'Read' the first two bars of music against the T,M,B,T pattern to see how the shorthand matches up.

Now listen to the next audio clip. A slight change to the bottom, middle, top order has been made. See if you can hear it.

min_02_02

41

The inside two notes in each broken chord have swapped places. The pattern now runs T, B, M, T instead of T, M, B, T – except for the last F chord, where T, B, M would not work (try it!). Play the pattern yourself.

Finally, here is an alternating pattern – one of each variety in turn.

min_02_03

It's a very small variation, but it stops the riff sounding mechanical.

To finish, the riff goes all the way from the top to the bottom. These are the chords and the final, alternating BMT pattern.

min_02_04

Play the simpler T, M, B, T or T, B, M, T variations if you prefer. The audio plays the pattern that's printed directly above. Repeat the whole riff, then repeat the last two chords as an outro/fade.

The i–♭VII broken chord riffs – Number 2

The more i–♭VII pairs you learn, the better you will grasp the pattern behind the music. The next riff is a syncopated i–♭VII broken chord pattern in E minor (i) and D (♭VII). Here is the audio clip.

min_02_05

You can hear that the right hand doesn't play notes every beat – there are gaps and notes played off the beat. The rhythm is 'syncopated'.

Here are the chords you need in a keyboard diagram. Remember that they could be higher or lower – the keyboards only show the shape of the chords.

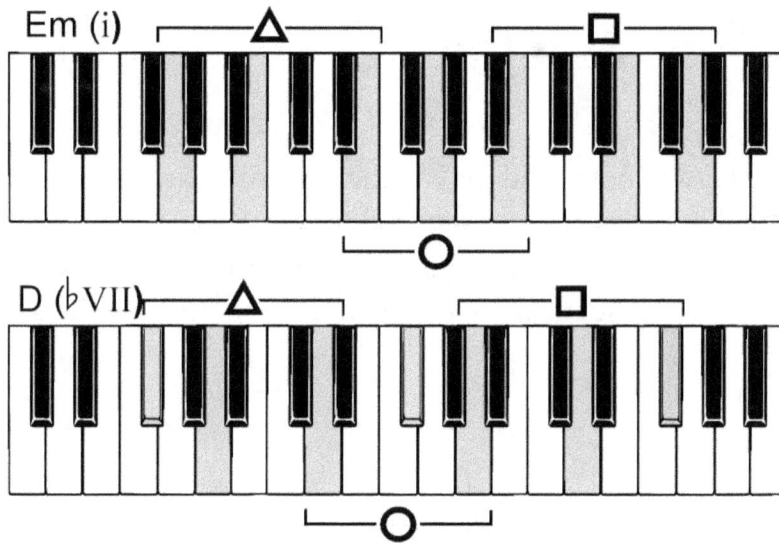

Find and rehearse the E minor and D triads.

The first two bars of the riff written out look like this.

Whenever you see music like this that you think might be a broken chord pattern, you should try to 'bunch it back up' (un-break it), so you can see what inversion is – like this.

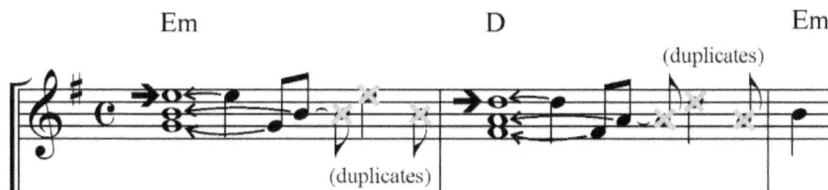

You see that both chords are first inversions, with the root (name-note) at the top. This is a much more creative way of reading music.

Then you look at the bottom, middle, top order ('BMT analysis').

Play that pattern. Get your fingers over the notes and look at them as you play top, bottom, middle, top, middle - in any rhythm. Do the same with the D chord.

Next, try to get the rhythm. If you're reading the music, you then see that there are tied notes and notes played off the beat, so you count the music out (in quavers), to see what beats the notes come on:

If you're working mainly by ear, you count one to eight quickly to yourself as you listen to the audio – so that each note gets a number of its own – and try and work out which of the eight beats don't have a note on them.

Counting one to eight evenly, you play the bottom, middle and top chord tones in the pattern you've identified. Practise repeating the first two chords first (E minor and D), then with the whole chord sequence.

These are the chords that, broken up, make the riff in the audio clip. The left hand (bass) notes (not shown) are the roots, with a note B on quaver count eight. Listen to the audio again and copy.

min_02_05

Of course, you have the option of copying the structure of the first riff in this module – play the first four chords twice, then run all the way from top to bottom, repeating the last two chords for a 'vamp' (holding pattern), then repeating the whole thing.

The i/♭VII broken chord riffs – Number 3

This riff is very similar to the last one, but we're going to learn it in the D minor-C i–♭VII pair of chords which you already know. Here are the inversions in a table. Find them and practice them.

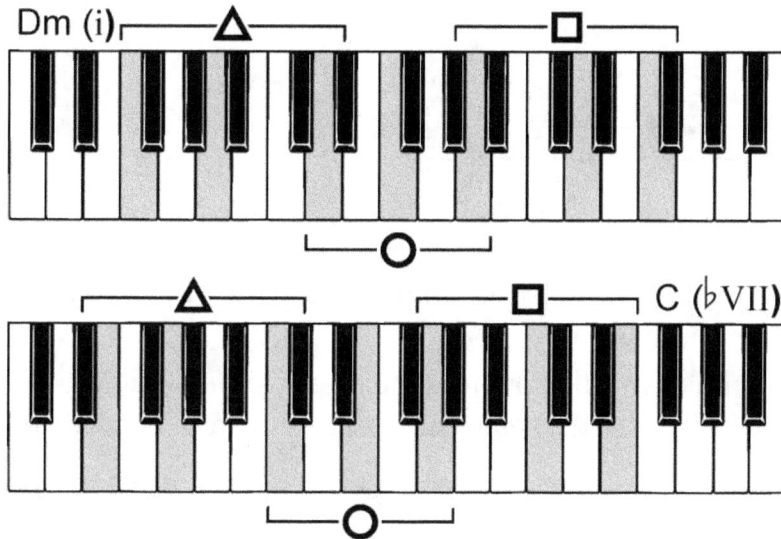

Here's the audio performance:

min_02_06

The first two bars of the riff that you hear, written out, look like this.

As before, you bunch the broken chord back up in your mind's eye (or ear!) so that you can identify the inversion and the BMT pattern:

It's a second inversion, represented by the square – the top two notes are closer to each other. (The other patterns so far have started with first inversions.) The name-note D is the middle

45

note. Put the third finger on D and the other notes (thumb and fifth finger) should find themselves.

There's a new symbol in this BMT pattern – 'O', for 'outside'. You play the outside notes of the chord – top and bottom – when you see 'O' in the BMT analysis.

But the right hand has a tricky rhythm. Count the audio riff out in quavers, one to eight. What counts do the notes come on?

Practice the rhythm on the right hand chords – copy the audio or skip down to the whole-riff chord sequence. Add a single-note (root) bass if you wish.

But we have to incorporate the bass line as well. Counting the bass, we find it comes on counts 1, 6 and 8, so the TLR (together, right, left) analysis is this (shown in between the staves).

It's always worth tapping out a complicated rhythm like this away from the keyboard (i.e. without notes involved) until you're quite comfortable with it before adding music to the mix.

Use the beat map audio to practise. Count yourself in and tap along, then tap to the music MS.

Audio only

The final diagram in this module shows all these things together. It's a picture of what good pop/rock keyboard players do when they make up catchy riffs like the one in the audio clip.

There's a lot of information here – don't be scared off! It's to read, not to play. Every bit of information here relates to a skill that's worth having, so read through the text blocks one at a time, slowly.

The chord symbol - D minor. The square symbol means 'second inversion' - the middle note (arrowed) is the root (name-note) D.

The BMT (bottom, middle, top) analysis - the order the three chord tones are played in. There's a new symbol - O for 'outside'. Play the two outside (top and bottom) notes of the chord when you see this symbol.

The chord in brackets is the 'bunched up' broken chord - which you instantly 'see' in the broken chord pattern. You don't play it, except as a broken chord.

You apply the pattern spelt out in the first two bars to the rest of the chords in the chord sequence.

The count, in quavers. Any quaver which doesn't have a note (including tied notes, e.g. beat 5 here) is in brackets.

The TLR (together, left, right) analysis. Shows you which hand(s) play(s) on the quaver beat above. Rehearse the pattern by tapping it out away from the keyboard.

Now, apply the pattern spelt out in these bars, as played in the audio clip, to the full chord sequence given here. The analysis has been left in the first two bars, as a reminder. The bass notes are roots, with A as the in-between note.

min_02_06

As always with the Musicarta riffs, it's fine if you just end up playing something similar or simpler. The point is to get a riff going and play it until your muscles remember it, as a foundation to build on.

THE AEOLIAN i-♭VII-♭VI

In this module, we're going to expand the i–♭VII pair we've been working with in the two previous modules into a three-chord Aeolian minor riff you're bound to recognize. This is the riff we build up to.

aeo_01_05

The i–♭VII–♭VI sequence

We're going to add another major chord one whole tone below the i–♭VII pairs we've been working with so far, which makes the new chord ♭VI ('flat six').

Listen to the familiar sound of this audio clip. The i–♭VII–♭VI sound is unmistakeable.

aeo_01_01

The roots of these next-door chords are a whole tone apart. (You want to know this so you can transpose the group of chords.)

- You have a minor chord – i
- A whole tone below that, you have a major chord – ♭VII
- Another whole tone below **that**, you have another major chord - ♭VI

Three-note chords (triads) can have any one of the three chord tones at the top. The chords in the first example are all first inversions (triangle symbol – root at the top). Here is the same chord sequence using second inversions as well (square symbol – third at the top)

aeo_01_02

48

As you can hear, nothing is more natural than to start slipping between inversions. (Listen out for what the bass does in bar 3.)

aeo_01_03

The one thing you want to avoid is using **only** root positions.

aeo_01_04

The outside notes are fifths, and this is too stark a sound to listen to for long. The audio clip tries to demonstrate this. (In classical music, these 'parallel fifths' are completely outlawed.) Besides, it sounds like you've never learnt your inversions!

The module riff

Listen to the module i–♭VII–♭VI riff again

aeo_01_05

You should recognise some of the techniques used. The chords are broken up into broken chord patterns – including the 'O' for 'outside' (top and bottom) voices. There are other things going on as well – new tricks to make your chords go further. Let's look in detail.

Here are the skeleton chords.

Am G F G Am F G

i   ♭VII   ♭VI   ♭VII   i   ♭VI   ♭VII

aeo_01_06

It's made up of parts of the previous examples. You should be able to piece it together. If you don't read music very well, use the circle-square-triangle symbols and the Musicarta Visual Glossary of chords or the illustrations with circle-square-triangle symbols in this workbook.

Here's a simple 'realisation' of the chord sequence.

Am G F G Am G

T B M T T B M T O ⇗ T O ⇗ T T

1 (2) (3) 4 5 (6) (7) 8

F G

1 (2) (3) 4 (5) (6) 7 (8)

aeo_01_07

The 'O' in the BMT analysis stands for 'outside' – you play the outside two notes of the triad only.

Errata: Under the new system of crotchet counting. The last two bars would be marked up 1 (& 2) & 3 (& 4) | 1 (& 2) & (3 &) 4 |.

Adding next-door notes

But what are the ? question mark notes in the BMT analysis? They are next-door notes. The note next door to any chord tone (B, M or T) is always a good bet to try for filling up more quaver slots. Then, all you need to know is – is it above (higher) or below (lower)? These 'question mark notes' are all above, so we can use an up arrow.

Our BMT analysis will then be as follows.

aeo_01_05

As well as 'O' for 'outside', there's a symbol 'C', for 'chord' – just play the whole chord on that beat.

The full set of BMT symbols is now:

Symbol	Stands for	Meaning
B	bottom	Play the lowest note of a three-note chord
M	middle	Play the middle note of a three-note chord
T	top	Play the highest note of a three-note chord
O	outside	Play the outside (top and bottom) notes of a three-note chord
C	chord	Play the whole chord (usually three notes)
↗	go up	Play the note one higher (in the scale) than the last top note

Notice that some chords are anticipated – played before their 'straight' beat. The chord symbols have been moved forward so that you can see, for example, that the second 'O' refers to the G chord.

Notice that the last F chord is slimmed down to just two notes, so 'C' ('Play the whole chord') means only two notes.

Adding the bass

Next, you need to look at how the proper riff bass (left hand) fits in with this right hand pattern. Read the following TLR (together, left, right) analysis carefully.

aeo_01_08

Because the right hand plays on nearly every quaver, it's not too difficult to see when to play the left hand notes.

Practice just the right hand, first two bars. Fill up bars three and four practising just the rhythm of the bass – here counted in eight quavers.

Bars 3 and 4 - the rhythm

The rhythm of the last two bars is complex. There are melody notes at the top and an internal rhythm played by the left hand and the inside fingers of the right hand.

The first step is to identify and practice the internal rhythm. Here's the beat map of the two bars, without the melody.

aeo_01_BM1 (audio only)

If necessary, just tap the TLR (together, left, right) events regardless of rhythm.

T   R   L   L   R   L   T   T   R   L

aeo_01_BM2 (audio only)

When you've got that, re-introduce the proper rhythm with just the 'inside' chords.

Am   G   F   G
1 (2) 3 4 5 6 (7) 8   1 (2 3) 4 (5) 6 7 (8)

T   R L L R   L   T   T   R L

aeo_01_09

Modern keyboard solo style – right hand – often needs you to play or hold a melody note at the top and play rhythm chords underneath. Here's a sample exercise for this key skill.

aeo_01_10

In case you're not good at reading leger lines, here's that right hand written an octave higher.

Then the last bar as written.

aeo_01_11

Finally, the anticipated melody note E.

53

aeo_01_12

The full module riff is intermediate-to-advanced – you can expect to have to have to come back to it a few times. The upside is, this 'messing about with chords' slowly builds into an enviable creative skill, and the simpler versions of the riff you learn in the process (Musicarta's 'stepping-stone performances') are good material in any event.

Finally, here's the riff MS in full.

aeo_01_05

Listen out for the Aeolian i–♭VII–♭VI group of chords in popular music of all kinds.

In the next module in this series, we transpose the i–♭VII–♭VI group of chords into two different keys. Transposing is a 'core' musical skill. The more you transpose, the more you understand the inner workings of popular music harmony and the easier it will be to let your creative ideas flow.

TRANSPOSING i-♭VII-♭VI

Transposing chord sequences is one of the key musical skills. If you can transpose chord sequences, you really do understand the 'inner workings' of music harmony, knowledge that puts you right at the front of the field.

Transposing i–♭VII–♭VI

Revise what you know about the i–♭VII–♭VI chord group.

In Aeolian One (module), we added a major chord one whole tone below the i–♭VII pairs we explored previously. This is the ♭VI ('flat six') chord.

The roots of these next-door i–♭VII–♭VI chords are a whole tone apart.

- You have a minor chord – i
- A whole tone below that, you have a major chord – ♭VII
- Another whole tone below **that**, you have another major chord - ♭VI

Three-note chords (triads) can have any one of the three chord tones at the top, making nine possible right hand chords in all.

Chords A minor, G and F are the only place on the keyboard you can find a i–♭VII–♭VI chord group using only the white keys. The two new i–♭VII–♭VI groups of chords explored in this module use one black key.

D minor, C and B flat

D minor, C and B♭ (majors) are another Aeolian i–♭VII–♭VI chord group. Here is a keyboard diagram of the three chords in all possible inversions.

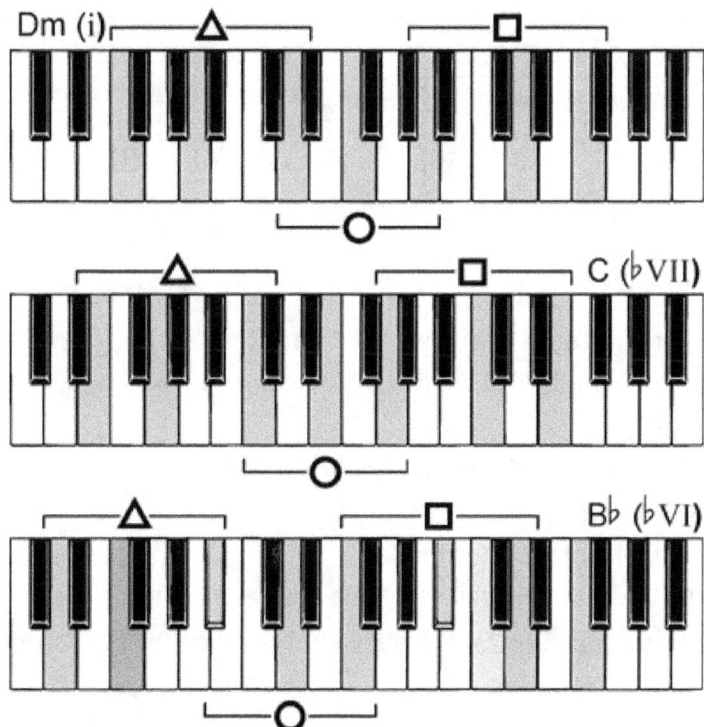

- D minor is our i (tonic, home) chord. The D minor chord is an all-white-key chord.
- Note C is a whole tone below D, and an all-white-key chord built on C is a major chord – our ♭VII.
- To drop a whole tone from C (to make our ♭VI chord), we have to go to black key B flat, and build our ♭VI (major) chord up from there. (There is no black key between white keys C and B on the keyboard, so they are only a semi-tone apart.)

Use the keyboard diagram to rehearse the three chords in all possible inversions.

Work those B♭ chords **a lot!** The notes look and feel a lot more evenly spaced than the other chords/inversions, and everybody finds the B♭ chords m a bit difficult at first.

The first module riff

Get to know the first module riff. It's essentially an accompaniment.

aeo_02_01

Here are the skeleton chords of the first part.

aeo_02_02

The right hand plays around middle C, which involves a lot of leger lines. The second half of the MS has the same music written an octave higher, with the *8vb* ('play an octave lower') indication.

Notice that these are all second inversion chords (square symbol, root/name note in the middle).

We will not be so concerned about playing the riff exactly as in the audio in this module. Find the inversions and play along, matching the rhythmic as well as you can.

The next audio track offers a slight variation. Can you hear what it is?

aeo_02_03

The right hand chord doesn't change when the bass note walks down in the first bar. You end up with what is called as 'slash chord'. Here's the music.

Not changing something you might expect to change, or that you changed before, is a powerful way of creating more music – and stopping things getting stale.

Explore the other inversions, as in the previous module. Logically you would get.

aeo_02_04

But you will remember in the previous module we said to avoid 'parallel fifths'. So we do the same kind of thing as before and keep the top right hand note the same as the notes underneath move.

aeo_02_05

There are still a lot of root position (circle symbol) chords there, but the variation makes it sound better.

The last inversion to explore is the lowest.

aeo_02_06

This is a very 'mixed bag'! You cannot take the first inversions down parallel – the sound is just too low. (You hear this group chords in the second half of the previous audio clip as well.)

If you play these three D minor i-♭VII-♭VI segments one after the other in the order they are presented in this module, you get a rhythm section backing for improvisation – or just a groove to get into. The last audio clip above goes back to the start and repeats in this way.

Second riff – E minor, D and C

E minor, D and C are another i-♭VII-♭VI group of chords that uses only one black key – in this case, F sharp.

In this section you will learn how to create simple variations built around this group of chords and make a solo of a decent length, and to get your hands so familiar with the chords and the types of movement that they themselves start coming up with ideas.

Listen to the 'wizards and princesses'-type riff we build on E minor, D and C in this section.

> aeo_02_07

Refer to the keyboards diagram on the next page for the inversion you will need.

Making accompaniment patterns from a triad

Let's focus on the accompaniment pattern first.

The basic 'seed' of most accompaniment patterns is the root position triad (the circle symbol chords in the keyboards diagram).

The root position triad uses the root, third and fifth (R, 3, 5) of some scale. These are the 'chord tones'.

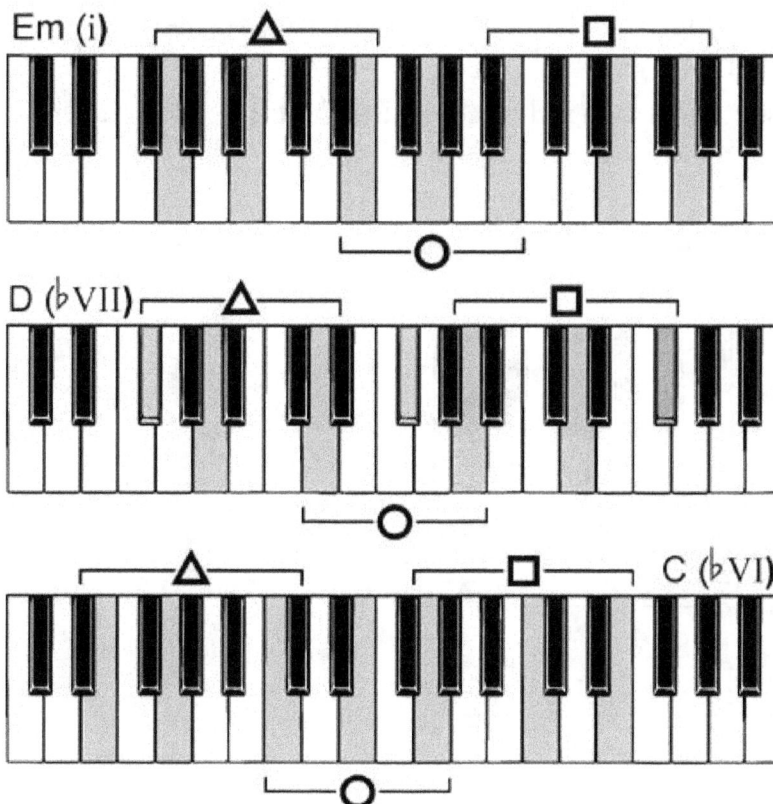

You can play the simple root position triad as an accompaniment, but the accompaniment patterns can be made a lot more interesting by:

- 'Doubling' (repeating) the root at the octave, which makes it '8', and

- Moving the third up an octave, where it becomes 'the tenth' ('10').

Here is that process shown on the keyboard, for E minor:

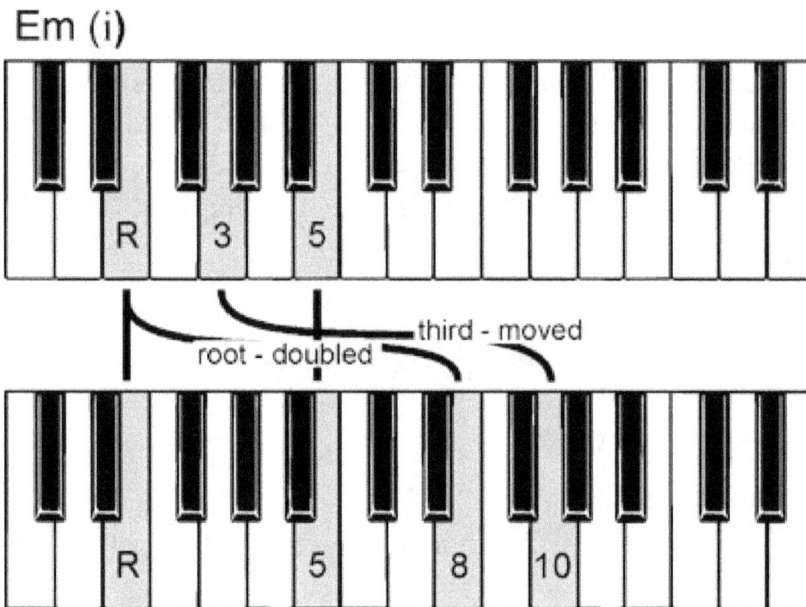

Em (i)

Do this with all three triads (as shown below). You can use two hands to play the accompaniment pattern (for now).

The audio clip demonstrates the process, and the root-fifth-octave-tenth (R-5-8-10) accompaniment pattern in all three chords.

The fifth, octave and tenth are here shown written in both the bass and treble clefs. These are the <u>same</u> <u>notes</u>.

aeo_02_08

Em (i)

D (♭VII)

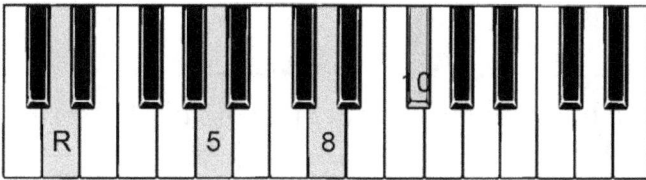

C (♭VI)

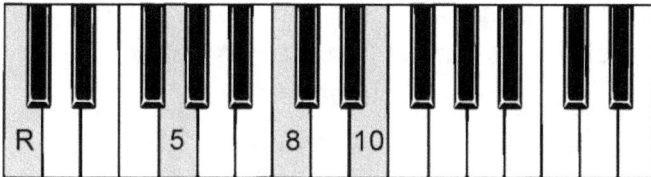

If you just played the notes up and down, you would get a pattern in six-eight. Here it is, using the same chord sequence as for the previous riff.

aeo_02_09

61

Take time to read the information around the notes – it shows how real musicians think when they 'just sit down and play', improvising riffs like this.

1. Below, you see the I–♭VII–♭VI coding. What this indicates is:

    "A minor chord (i) with a major chord a whole tone below (♭VII) and another major chord a whole tone below that (♭VI)."

2. At the top, you see the conventional chord symbols. Given any particular minor chord – in this case, E minor - top musicians will be able to hear the possibility of a I–♭VII–♭VI sequence and will know what the ♭VII and ♭VI chords will be (D and C majors, in this case). You should expect to be able to do the same – it sounds more complicated that it is!

3. You also see the inversion symbol – all squares, for second inversions (root in the middle).

    You will normally avoid parallel root positions because of the harsh 'parallel fifths' (first example, below). Parallel first inversions aren't very interesting because the top note is the same as the bass note (the root) (second example below).

    The parallel tenths sound you get from second inversions with the third, or tenth, at the top) is the nicest (third example). This is not a hard and fast rule – see if you agree!

aeo_02_10

4. Also above the music is the 'BMT analysis'. This tells you the order in which the bottom, middle and top right hand inversion notes are used to fill up the bar.

5. In between the staves you see the chord tone shorthand – root, fifth, octave and tenth (R-5-8-10). Our 'top musician' knows to use these notes in broken chord patterns selected according to the style of music from a 'memory bank' of accompaniment patterns (like this one) built up over the years. He or she knows the chord, selects the inversions and 'waggles the fingers' according to the pattern they have in mind.

    Work through the process often enough and you'll do that too!

Make the accompaniment pattern (repeated below) as beautiful as you can. Music doesn't have to be complex to be beautiful, but you do have to decide to make it beautiful.

Make the bass line sing out. Make the highest notes stand out with a bit of extra 'push' and play them 'sticky' to make them last longer.

aeo_02_09

The accompaniment pattern above uses both hands. That's fine if you just want to 'strum' the piano and wait for ideas, or accompany someone. But if you're going to play a melody as well, you have to play the accompaniment with one hand.

It's easy to do if you get the fingering right.

aeo_02_11

As you can see, it's a simple formula.

LH fingering			
5	2	1	2
Root (R)	Fifth (5)	Octave (8)	Tenth (10)

Then, as pointed out in bullet point 3 above, some tune built on the tenths will sound good. The following music MS and sound clip demonstrate.

aeo_02_12

The tenths, now in the right hand and at the start of each bar, are joined by little two-note runs of next-door notes. Next door can be either up or down. The arrows show which way you move – up or down. The second time these four bars of music appear the up/down profile is slightly different. This makes the music more interesting for the listener.

The right hand thumb joins in with a few notes. The left hand carries on playing the accompaniment pattern. You hear all this in the audio clip above.

Of course, you can always play just chord tones in the right hand. Try following this BMT analysis (second inversion chords throughout):

aeo_02_13

The audio has the left hand accompaniment carrying on underneath, but the right hand part sounds good over simple bass notes. Listen to the following sample. Count off the six quavers in the bar and decide where the bass (left hand) notes – all roots – come.

aeo_02_14 (audio only)

Next, we combine part of the broken chord pattern with the melody.

aeo_02_15

Next, the melody appears at the bottom of the right hand, with the added notes above. You have to be clever to keep you two hands out of each other's way.

aeo_02_16

The audio clip fades out with this advanced tuplet figure.

R 5 8 10 8 5   R 5 8 R 5 8

aeo_02_17

Substitute something simpler if this is too difficult for you right now.

Listen to the full riff audio again and copy the ending.

In this module you have seen how:

- A simple chord can be expanded into a broken chord accompaniment and a chord sequence played using the pattern;
- A melody can be made by stringing chord tones together with varied next-door note patterns;
- Broken chord figures can be played in the treble (right hand) over broken chords in the left hand as well;
- The same music played an octave higher or lower is not a boring repetition, but can easily sound like new material altogether;
- These variations can be strung together to make a decent length solo with the promise of more to come!
- The Aeolian mode provides a trio of chords (I–♭VII–♭VI) that is ideal for improvisations of this sort.

In the next module, you will practise harmonising tunes with the three Aeolian chords you know, and learn new techniques for putting together great riffs. You will be amazed at how much music three simple chords can generate!

HARMONISING WITH i-♭VII-♭VI

This Musicarta Modes workbook module practises harmonising using the rich Aeolian three-chord set explored in Aeolian Modules One and Two.

Harmonising at the keyboard

The essence of the practical musician's skill is to find chords from a certain set – usually a key but in this case a modal chord family – to harmonise a melody. By 'harmonise', we mean "find a chord which 'supports' the melody note" – and hang it underneath that note. The melody note will be the top of the three chord tones.

The top line/melody to harmonise is this.

aeo_03_01

Our key is A Aeolian, and for the moment we will use just the I–♭VII–♭VI Aeolian set of three chords from the previous modules. In A Aeolian, I–♭VII–♭VI are A minor, G and F majors.

Think about which chords to use to harmonise the top line given.

- The first note is C. Note C is a chord tone of both the F (major) and A minor chords in our set. You can harmonise C with either an A minor or an F chord – that is, you can hang either an A minor or an F major chord underneath the note C.
- The next note is B. Only chord G from our limited Aeolian set has B as a chord tone. The chord must be G.
- The next note, A, can be harmonised with either an A minor or an F chord.
- The next note, E, can only be harmonised with an A minor chord (out of our limited set).
- The next note, D, can only be harmonised with a G chord.
- The next note, C, can be harmonised with either an A minor or an F chord.
- The last note is B, which can only be harmonised with the G chord.

So the possibilities are:

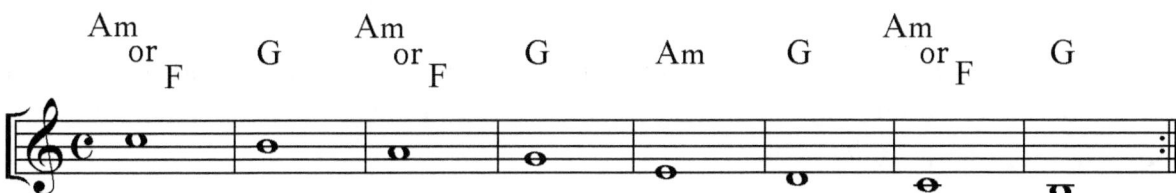

67

Let's work with just four possibilities to start with.

Top note	c	b	a	g	e	d	c	b
1.	Am □	G □	F □	G △	Am ○	G ○	F ○	G □
or
2.	F ○	G □	Am △	G △	Am ○	G ○	F ○	G □
or
3.	F ○	G □	F □	G △	Am ○	G ○	Am □	G □
or
4.	Am □	G □	Am △	G △	Am ○	G ○	F ○	G □

aeo_03_02	aeo_03_03	aeo_03_04	aeo_03_05

Your first job is to find inversions of those chords – including the alternatives for melody notes A and C – which have our melody notes at the top. Play along with the audio files. Read the next section also for help, if needed.

Using inversion symbols to help

The circle/square/triangle inversion symbols help you think about what shape your right hand should make.

Think it through. Your right hand only plays three chord shapes – root position, first inversion or second inversion. As we are in A Aeolian – which only uses the white piano keys – we can find our chord shapes with "play one, miss one, play one" white-key counting.

Look at this diagram.

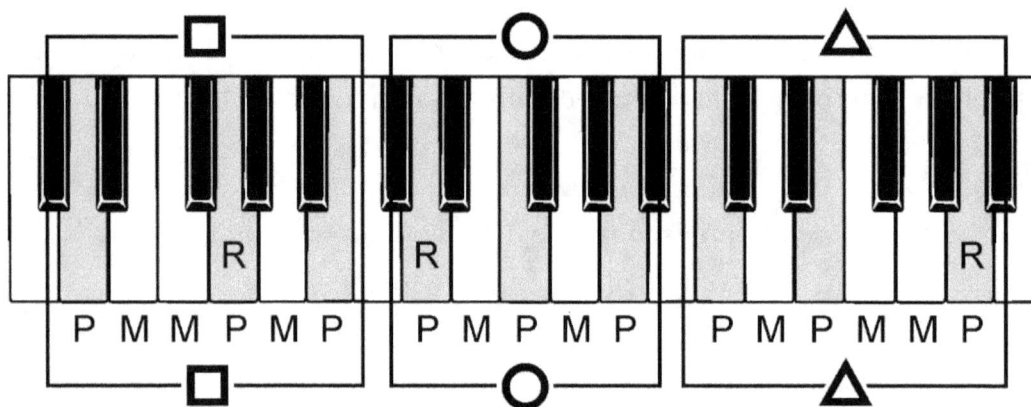

P stands for 'play'. M stands for 'miss'. We are not interested in what actual chords these are. We are only interested in their 'play one, miss one, play one' shape.

Read through the following statements.

- Any two triad chord tones in A Aeolian (an all-white-key mode) have either one or two missed white keys between them – P M P or P M M P (Miss, Play).
- Triad chord tones are either equally spaced – the play one, miss one, play one, miss one, play one root position chord, **or**
- One pair of notes is closer together (play one, miss one, play one) and the other note is two missed keys away – a first or second inversion chord.
- The root position chord covers five white keys; the two other inversions cover six white keys.

Here is that information in a table:

Symbol	Inversion	Shape	Note spacing
△	First inversion	o← 8	The bottom two notes are closest together (low) **P M P M M P** (high)
O	Root position	8 8←	The notes are equally spaced **P M P M P**
□	Second inversion	8← o	The top two notes are closest together **P M M P M P**

The name-note (or root – arrowed in the table) is the capital letter in the chord symbol. It's either the top (first inversion), the bottom (root position), or the middle note (second inversion) of a triad.

In this riff, the melody note is always the top note of the three-note chord. Put your right hand little finger on the melody note and try the three shapes. One will have the chord name-note in the right place. That's your chord.

Here are the four chord sequences repeated for your convenience:

(1)   Am □   G □   F □   G △   Am O   G O   F O   G □

or

(2)   F O   G □   Am △   G △   Am O   G O   F O   G □

or

(3)   F O   G □   F □   G △   Am O   G O   Am □   G □

or

(4)   Am □   G □   Am △   G △   Am O   G O   F O   G □

aeo_03_02	aeo_03_03	aeo_03_04	aeo_03_05

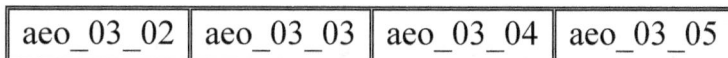

Play along with the four chord-sequence audio clips using just plain block chords, then go on to the next section.

Whole-bar BMT variations

Our chord sequence has the chords lasting a whole bar – four crotchet or eight quaver counts. Broken chord patterns are usually quaver patterns. The simplest broken chord patterns have right hand quavers on every count, making a total of eight quavers to the bar.

Pattern 1

Here's a broken chord pattern to use on Chord Sequence 1.

Top note	c	b	a	g	e	d	c	b
1.	Am □	G □	F □	G △	Am ○	G ○	F ○	G □

The pattern is T B M B T B M T – shown here for any second inversion chord (root arrowed. The stave lines have been taken away to help you think of this as 'a pattern anywhere'.

aeo_03_06

In the audio performance, the first four bars have a pedal bass note A; the other four bass notes are all roots. Simplify the tricky bass rhythm if you like.

Pattern 2

Here's another BMT pattern, used on Chord Sequence (3).

Top note	c	b	a	g	e	d	c	b
3.	F ○	G □	F □	G △	Am ○	G ○	Am □	G □

The pattern is T M B T M B M T – shown here for any second inversion chord (root arrowed).

aeo_03_07

The audio performance uses a pedal bass note A all the way through.

Pattern 3

Once there are gaps – quaver slots with no notes – the rhythm is 'syncopated'. Here is a syncopated pattern from the Minor Modes (2) module.

Em   D   Em
T   B M   T   M   T   B M   T   M

1 (2) 3 4 (5) 6 (7) 8 | 1 (2) 3 4 (5) 6 (7) 8

min_02_05

If you apply that texture to our Chord Sequence 1, you will get something like this.

aeo_03_08

Pattern 4

Also from Minor Modes (2):

Dm   O   M B   M T   C   O   M B   M T

1 (2) 3 4 (5) 6 7 8   1 (2) 3 4 (5) 6 7 8
T   R R   T R L   T   R R   T R L

min_02_06

If you apply that pattern to Chord Sequence (2), you will get the following music.

Top note	c	b	a	g	e	d	c	b
2.	F ○	G □	Am △	G △	Am ○	G ○	F ○	G □

aeo_03_09

Minim BMT variations

The chords could change twice as quickly, using two chords in each bar. Each chord will then only have four quaver beats.

Pattern 5

Here is a two-chords-per-bar pattern using Chord Sequence 1.

Am □ G □   F □ G △   Am ○ G ○   F ○ G □
T M B T   B M T   T M B T   B M T   T M B   T   B M T   T M B T   B M T

Listen to the audio file and see if you can play it.

| aeo_03_10 |

Note that the BMT analysis is simplified a little – some additional chord tones are 'thrown in'. The BMT analysis refers to the top notes of the triads. You will start to fill out the patterns with extra chord tones as you understand the technique better – and you can get your fingers there in time.

Note also that the second chord in each bar is always anticipated (brought forward a quaver – your ear should tell you). The chord symbols have been brought forward over their actual T (for top note) symbol to help you (this wouldn't normally be the case).

Pattern 6

Try learning the next pattern from just the BMT analysis and the audio.

Am□ G□   F□ G△   AmO GO   FO   G□
B T M O   T M B   B T M O   T M B M B T M   B T   M B T T   M B

| aeo_03_11 |

This uses our Chord Sequence 1 as well.

Remember: 'O' stands for 'outside' – play the top and bottom (outside) notes of the three-note inversion indicated by the circle/square/triangle symbol.

Here's the music for the example:

Am□ G□   F□ G△   AmO GO   FO   G□
B T M O   T M B   B T M O   T M B M B T M   B T   M B T T   M B

Mixing Patterns and Chord Sequences

Try applying Pattern 6 to Chord Sequence 3

FO G□   F□ G△   AmO GO   Am□ G□
B T M O   T M B   B T M O   T M B M B T M   B T   M B T T   M B

| aeo_03_12 |

Here's the music for that version.

Experiment! Feel free to make any alterations 'good taste' seems to require.

Here's a version of that riff which is slightly 'tweaked', to deal with some harshness in the last bar. Can you hear what's happened?

aeo_03_13

Melodic variation

As well as making variations by experimenting with rhythmic broken chord patterns, we can make the melody line more interesting by using next-door notes, as we did in the Aeolian Two module.

The previous module's riff uses the present module's Chord Sequence 1.

Am □   G □   F □   G △   Am ○   G ○   F ○   G □

For melodic variation, it uses only the next note above the top chord tone. If we want to use the next note down as well, we need a down-arrow symbol as well. Our full set of symbols will therefore be:

Symbol	Stands for	Meaning
B	bottom	Play the lowest note of a three-note chord
M	middle	Play the middle note of a three-note chord
T	top	Play the highest note of a three-note chord
O	outside	Play the outside – top and bottom - notes of a three-note chord
C	chord	Play the whole chord (usually three notes)
⬀	go up	Play the note one higher (in the scale) than the last top note
⬂	go down	Play the note one lower (in the scale) than the last top note

(The new symbol is at the bottom.)

To recap, the Chord Sequence 1 chords are:

aeo_03_02

For now, we are just interested in the right hand, and we want to separate (in our mind) the top ('melody') note from the other two chord tones.

aeo_03_14

Now suppose we play around, using next door notes to get from one top note to the next. We can go up or down. Here's one possibility – without thinking about the rhythm, for the moment.

aeo_03_15

Use the fingering given so that you don't keep running out of fingers. Playing like this at the little-finger side of your right hand is essential in the modern keyboard style.

The actual performance (in the next audio clip) uses this rhythm all the way through.

Here's a melodic variation on a new chord sequence.

Practice using the next-door note melodic variation technique on the other module chord sequences. Feel free to change a note or two here or there in any of the examples, to satisfy your discriminating musical ear!

The last two modules in the Musicarta Modes workbook have taken time out from adding new chords to our modal set to show you how you can get the most out of the chords you have learned.

This is the method that has been demonstrated.

- You take a simple set of chords and use the inversions to put together a chord-sequence with a smooth and interesting top-line melody.

- You apply broken-chord patterns, with an interesting rhythm, to the chords in the chord sequence. This is often enough to make great music out of the bare chords.

- You can make further variations by joining the main melody notes with little next-door-note figures. You can also combine the broken chord and next-door note techniques.

If you want to get to a point where you can sit down at the keyboard and this 'just happens', play (and transpose!) the examples given here over and over.

Try to make slight variations on them by changing the chords or inversions; changing the broken chord pattern; and changing the up/down shape of the next-door-note connecting patterns.

ADDING AEOLIAN V ("FIVE MINOR")

In this module, we add chord 'v' ("Five minor") to our A Aeolian mode i-♭VII-♭VI ("One minor, Flat Seven, Flat Six") set. In A Aeolian the new chord is E minor.

The module riffs

This module's riffs settle the new Five minor chord in by rehearsing One minor-Five minor (i-v) chord changes in our familiar A Aeolian minor. It comes in three progressive versions, so you'll be sure to take away something from the module.

aeo_04_02	aeo_04_11	aeo_04_10

The expanded Aeolian chord set

Here is the expanded set of A Aeolian chords shown on keyboards. The new chord (E minor) is at the bottom.

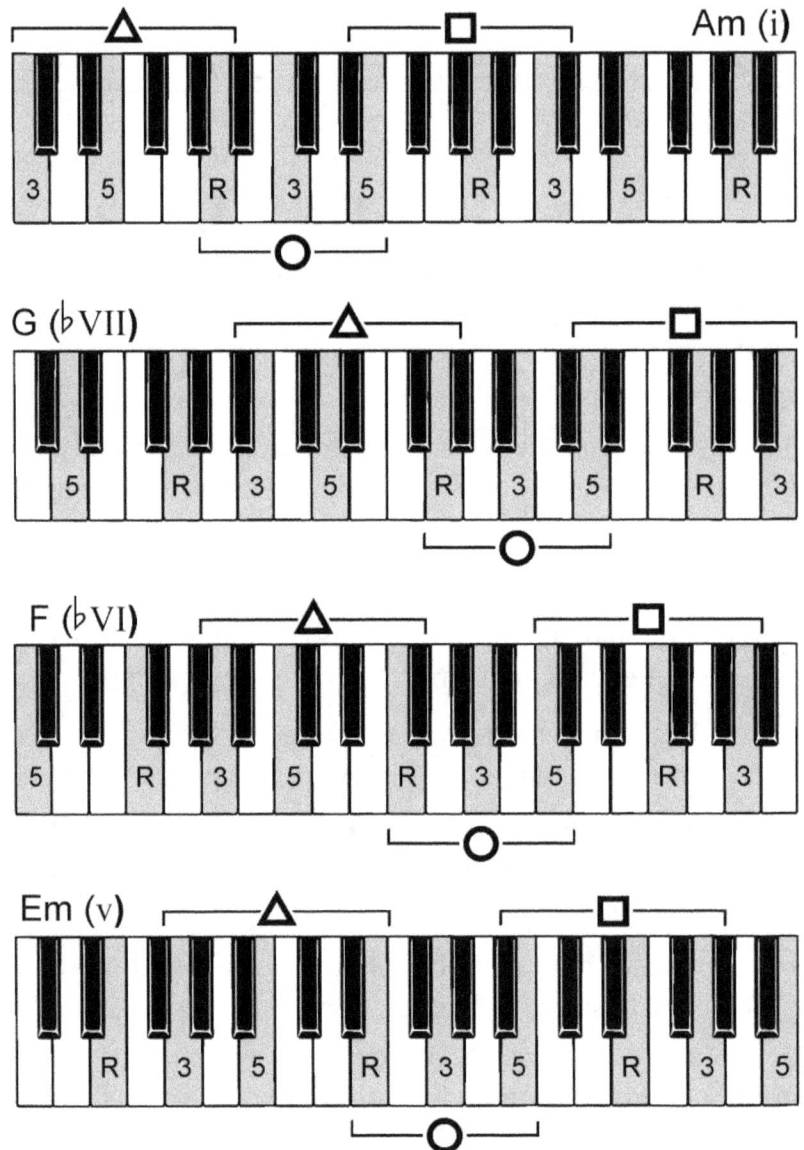

Look carefully at the new E minor chord tones. There is only one key different to the ♭VII G major chord – the note D in the G chord moves one step to note E in the E minor chord.

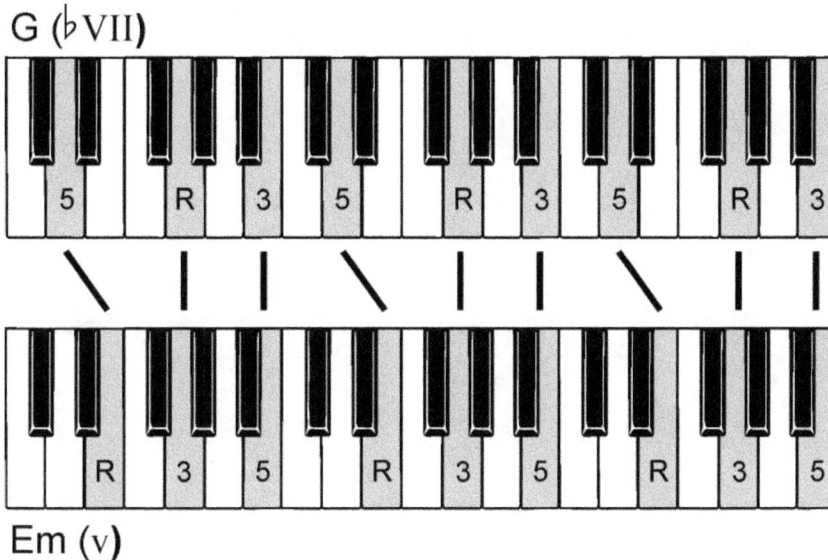

G (♭VII)

Em (v)

This means that you can use the new E minor chord to harmonise two notes (B and G) where you used the G chord before.

Use E minor chords where possible in the following chord sequence.

Find the inversions of the chords indicated which have the notes shown at the top. The circle/square/triangle symbols should help you. Refer to the Musicarta Keyboard Chord Generator or the labelled keyboard graphics in this workbook for help finding particular inversions.

Play six-eight TMB (top, middle , bottom) broken chord patterns all the way through with a simple one-note root in the bass and you will have something like this.

aeo_04_01

This is a very basic exercise which you will find easy to improve on.

Developing the melody

As in previous modules, we are going to use next-door notes to make the melody more interesting

!! IMPORTANT NOTE !! Simply **look at** the following examples. Save your energy and DO NOT play them, unless it's really easy for you!

The arrows indicate whether you move up (to the next white key up) or down.

We are going to do the same in this module. Our rhythm is six eight - the same as the first example above. Here is a sketch of what we want. Listen to the audio while you look at the music until you can hear the up/down melodic profile.

aeo_04_02

You will notice a new arrow symbol ⇨ which points straight to the side and means 'repeat the same note'.

Now, combine the developed melody and the six-eight TMB broken chord pattern, as in the audio clip above. Wherever there is a melody note, play it instead of the broken chord pattern note. On the first beat of the bar, they're the same note anyway.

Here's the written-out music for that clip. Make a good effort at putting the performance together from the instructions before you fall back on it.

This is what you hear in the audio clips above. The stems-up notes are the melody; the stems down notes are the TMB broken chord pattern

A left-hand accompaniment pattern

Next, make a left-hand accompaniment pattern and leave just the melody in the right hand.

In module Aeolian Two, we made a left hand accompaniment pattern in E minor out of a simple triad.

We 'doubled the root' to add another note at the octave, and shifted the third up an octave, making it 'the tenth'.

Do the same with an A minor triad. Start in the octave below middle C so our accompaniment pattern ends up in the right place. Use two hands to follow the audio.

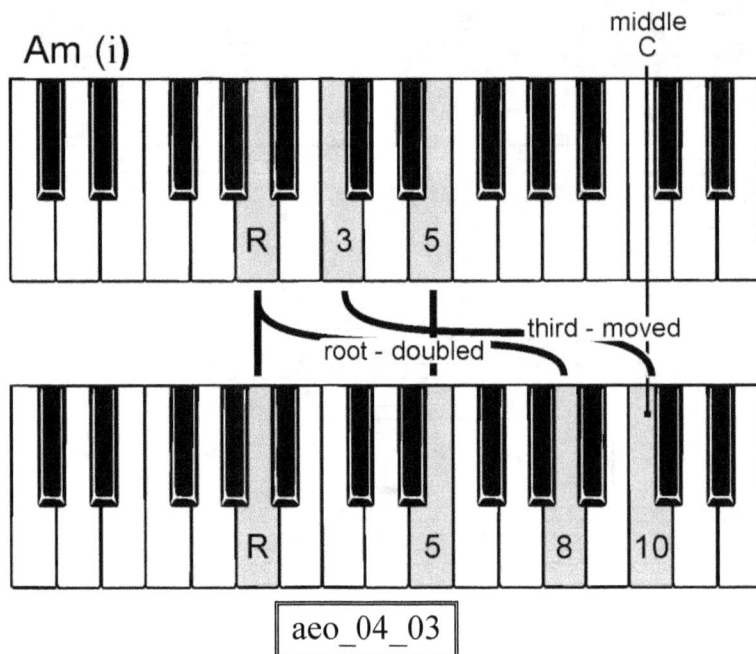

aeo_04_03

The written-out music for the six-eight pattern in the audio clip is as follows.

Am

R   5   8   10   8   5

(The fingering given is for left hand solo. You can play the pattern with two hands if you want, for now.)

The same accompaniment pattern in E minor is too low for this piece, so we use a different pattern for the E minor bars. You just add another root, an octave below, to a simple E minor triad.

aeo_04_04

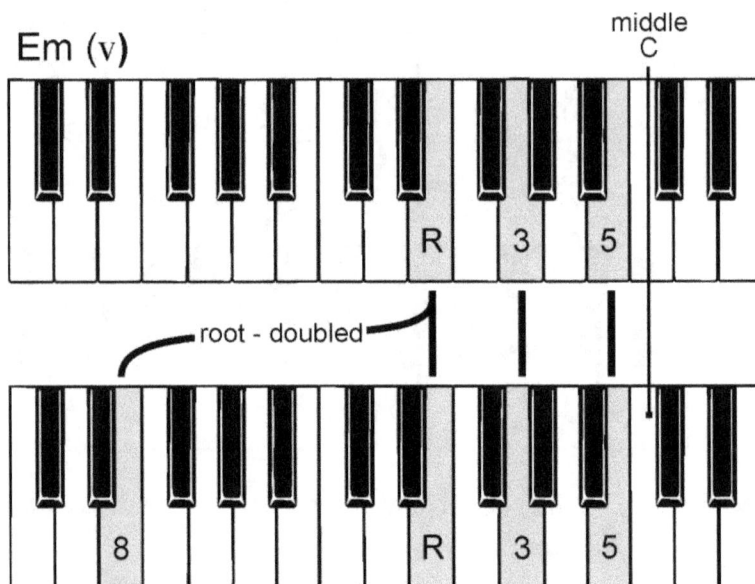

With this E minor accompaniment pattern, the two left hand chords are close to each other – and, in music, close to each other is 'a good thing'.

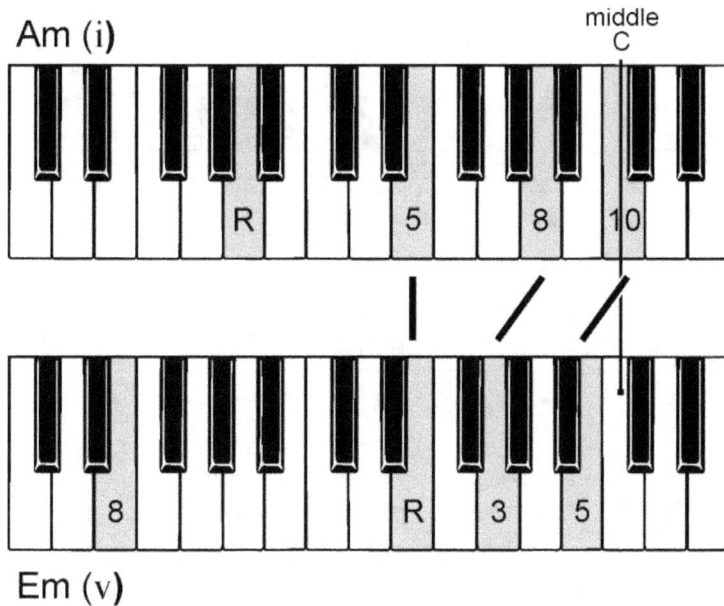

You see the voice movement diagram (between the keyboards) showing how the A minor triad changes into the E minor triad and back. The top two notes change, the bottom one stays the same.

Here is the music for the alternating i-and-v chord accompaniment pattern we use for the module riff.

R   5   8   10   8   5   8   R   3   5   3   R

aeo_04_05

Note: Easier accompaniment patterns are given further on, so you will be able to play the module riff even if you can't manage this pattern.

Practising the accompaniment pattern

The new accompaniment pattern is really only playable with the fingering given, so study it closely and then practice efficiently.

In left hand accompaniment patterns, you often have to move your hand quite quickly far beyond what it can stretch. In this case, the leap is from finger 2 on E, down an octave to finger 5 on the next E down (circled in the MS above).

Practice 'throwing' your hand that octave distance – from finger 2 to finger 5. The octave leap is always the same size and 'practice makes perfect'. Here are some exercises to help you.

aeo_04_06

Practise a little every day. Try it with your eyes closed – you don't see the pop pros staring at their hands! Listen carefully and learn from your mistakes. It's like practising any sporting skill.

Playing from a lead sheet

Now that you have accompaniment patterns in six-eight for chords A minor and E minor, you can play from a 'lead sheet' version of our riff, which shows only the melody and chord symbols.

Here is the lead sheet music, showing only the main chord tones.

For each chord symbol, you play one accompaniment pattern. Listen to the audio file and copy the performance. Play as slowly as you like to start with.

You should hear something like this.

aeo_04_09

Now play the developed melody in the right hand over the new left hand accompaniment pattern.

aeo_04_10

You will hear that the audio track has a four-bar Am-Em intro.

The cross-head notes in the MS are 'any note' notes – the ones you have to find by going up or down. THEY ARE NOT NECESSARILY WRITTEN IN THE RIGHT PLACE.

Try to find the melody notes using the shorthand sketch before you look at the following written-out music.

If you want, you can practice the improved melody over a simplified left hand accompaniment pattern. (Use this pattern anyway if you find the big one too difficult.)

aeo_04_11

You see what the simplified left hand accompaniment pattern is – root position triads broken up bottom, middle, top (BMT) over and over. (This is the left hand used in Riff Two in the audio table at the start of the module.)

Change the melody target tones

Now try to play the following melody line from the sketch and the audio file alone. The main ('target') notes are given. Use the simplified left hand (as written) or the full left hand pattern – the audio clip demos both.

aeo_04_12

Using the same rhythm, it easy to 'wander about' the keyboard heading for chord tone target notes. Try to re-create the following audio example from this sketch.

aeo_04_13

You will notice that this melody line requires the new symbol – the flat arrow, meaning 'repeat the same note'.

You don't have to stray so high if you don't want to. Here's a one-octave version to practice on.

aeo_04_14

(The MIDI file demos both types of left hand accompaniment.) Here is a version of the same melody which strays just a bit above and below the octave mark.

aeo_04_15

Here's another clip that just wanders between target A minor/E minor chord tones using the same two-moving-notes pattern. See if you can pick it up just from the audio clip.

aeo_04_16

Improvisation exercise

Let yourself go and see if you can wander between A minor and E minor chord tones using the pattern we've been practising – six-eight left hand broken chord accompaniment and two right hand moving motes at the end of the bar.

The Aeolian Four-Chord Set

This module rehearses the four chords in the Aeolian minor mode we have now built up.

The module riffs

The riffs in this module are in a more rocky four-four meter. The second example is a backing groove for improvising over, and explores 'slash bass' chords – chords with a note other than the root in the bass/left hand. This simple technique gives your riffs a sophisticated sound with no additional effort or theory background.

Here are the audio clips.

aeo_05_01	aeo_05_05

To start with, you will be using all four chords in the existing A Aeolian set, as shown in the top line of the table.

Aeolian minor	i 'One Minor'	♭VII 'Flat Seven'	♭VI 'Flat Six'	v 'Five Minor'
A	A minor	G	F	E minor
D	D minor	C	B♭	A minor
G	G minor	F	E♭*	D minor
E	E minor	D	C	B minor*

The other three sets of chords are shown to help you transpose our module chord sequences into other keys. When you transpose, you really get to think about how music is put together.

The chords marked with an asterisk – E flat and B minor – have not been shown on keyboards in this series yet. Use the Musicarta Keyboard Chord Generator to find them if you need help.

Don't forget to look at the Roman numerals in the table and in the music from time to time. If you think about chords in Roman numerals, you learn not just one chord sequence but many, and put your hands on the levers of a powerful music-making machine.

Here are the A Aeolian chords we will be working with, shown on keyboards. They should be quite familiar to you by now.

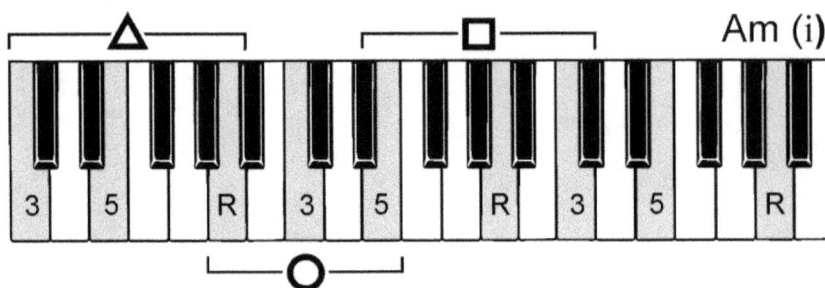

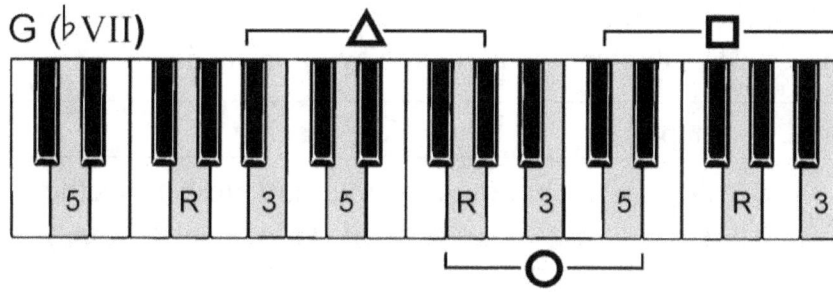

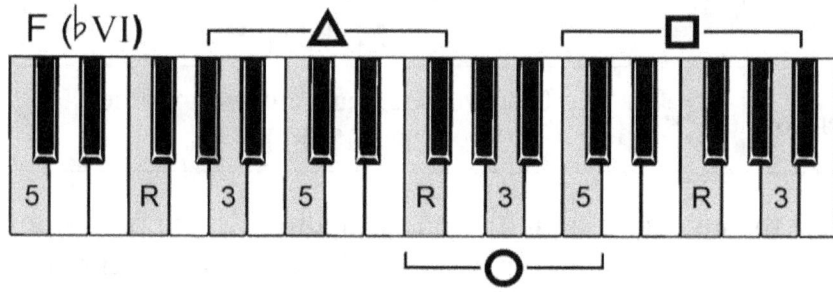

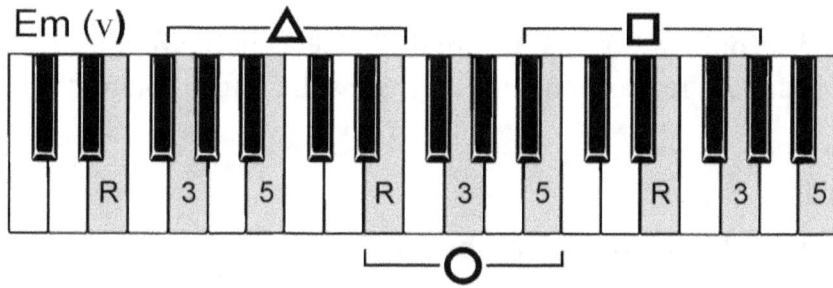

Riff One

Here are the top notes of the first riff chords. Use the inversion symbols (circle, square, triangle) to help you find them.

aeo_05_02

87

The riff is in A Aeolian – an all-white-key mode, so you can use simple play one, miss one (P, M) key counting to find the chords. Here are the inversion symbols again.

Symbol	Inversion	Shape	Note spacing
△	First inversion	o 8	The bottom two notes are closest together (low)　　P M P M M P　　(high)
O	Root position	8	The notes are equally spaced P M P M P
□	Second inversion	8 o	The top two notes are closest together P M M P M P

Try to find the chords using just the inversion symbols and the audio file, and play along to practice the inversions. If you need it, the written-out skeleton chords are at the end of the module.

Notice how the top notes of the second half of the riff are the same as in the first half – but the chords are different. This is called 'reharmonising'. It makes the music sound more interesting.

Riff One with broken chords

Here is a BMT sketch of the audio clip performance which follows.

Remember, C stands for 'chord', meaning play all the notes of the chord at once.

Errata The last (Am) inversion symbol on each line is wrong – they should be switched.

Here is just the right hand TMB broken chord patterning.

aeo_05_03

88

The last two bars

Rehearse the rhythm of the last two bars in each half by tapping out this beat map.

1   2 & 3   &(4)&   1   2 & 3   4

T   R L   T   R   R   L   R L   R   R
164

The first of these tapping audio files is at practice speed; the second is *a tempo*.

| aeo_05_BM1 (audio only) | aeo_05_BM2 (audio only) |

Listen to the riff audio clip again and tap along with the last two bars in each half.

1 (2)& 3 (4)&   1 2 & 3 4   1 2&3 4   1 2&3 4   1 (2)& 3 (4)&

L   LL   R   L R L R R   L RLR R   L RLR R   L   LL   R

| aeo_05_04 |

Here is a keyboard exercise for the same part, where the right hand splits into 'lead' and 'rhythm' sections. The right-hand side of the hand (finger 5) plays and holds the melody note while right hand fingers 1 and 3 (the cross-head notes in the beat map) keep chopping out the chords.

Here is the Riff One audio again, to check your version of the last two bars.

| aeo_05_01 |

Riff Two: Slash bass chords

A slash bass chord is a chord with a note other than the root (name-note) in the bass –in the left hand, for keyboard players. Slash chords often result from the bass line being 'smoothed out'. Slash chords make music sound more sophisticated – for no extra effort – and multiply the variety of sounds you can get out of any one chord sequence.

Here, the A minor/E minor/F chord sequence (i–v–♭VI) is explored in three places, starting on each of the three inversions of the A minor chord. Listen to the difference between these two versions of the same chord changes.

aeo_05_06

In the first two bars of each line, the bass is the root (name-note). It has to leap beyond the F then step back to arrive at the F chord bass note.

In the second two bars of each line, the bass moves smoothly by steps. It can do this because the bass note G is an E minor chord tone. The smooth bass line creates the slash chord, Em/G – "E minor over G", or "E minor with G in the bass".

Notice that:

- The circle/square/triangle symbols do not change because of the slash bass. Circle/square/triangle symbols tell us only about the three-note right hand chords (triads).

- The Roman numerals do not change because of the slash bass.

These chords make a good backing groove for soloing over. The three positions – starting on higher and higher inversions of A minor – provide a good device for building intensity.

Here's the music and an audio performance of a slash-bass backing groove on i, v, ♭IV.

| aeo_05_07 | aeo_05_08 | aeo_05_09 |

The syncopation in the actual-performance module Riff Two varies. The three practice segments above – with respective MIDI clips – offer an opportunity to 'zoom in' at practice speed to really perfect a two0handed pattern.

Here is a simplified pattern written out, with a practice-speed audio clip, to get you started.

aeo_05_10

When you are moving as many different inversions as this around, it is essential that you analyze voice movement – which notes in the chord move, and how. If you study the voice movement diagrams conscientiously, your chord work will improve dramatically.

Notice how an in-between inversion of chord G is used at the end of each in the sketch-music example above to transition between the groups of Am–Em–F inversions – a little extra trick worth working out.

Here are the written out chords for the first module riff.

aeo_05_02

The fingering (previous page) is for a very legato performance.

Here is the module riff written out in full.

aeo_05_01

AEOLIAN FIVE-CHORD SET (PART 1)

Stage One: Adding ♭III

The next chord we add to the Aeolian family is ♭III ("Flat Three"). ♭III is a major chord built on the note three semitones up from the mode's name-note (the tonic). In A Aeolian, ♭III is C major.

Listen to the recorded performance of the module riff.

aeo_06_01

The chords you will need are on this group of keyboards.

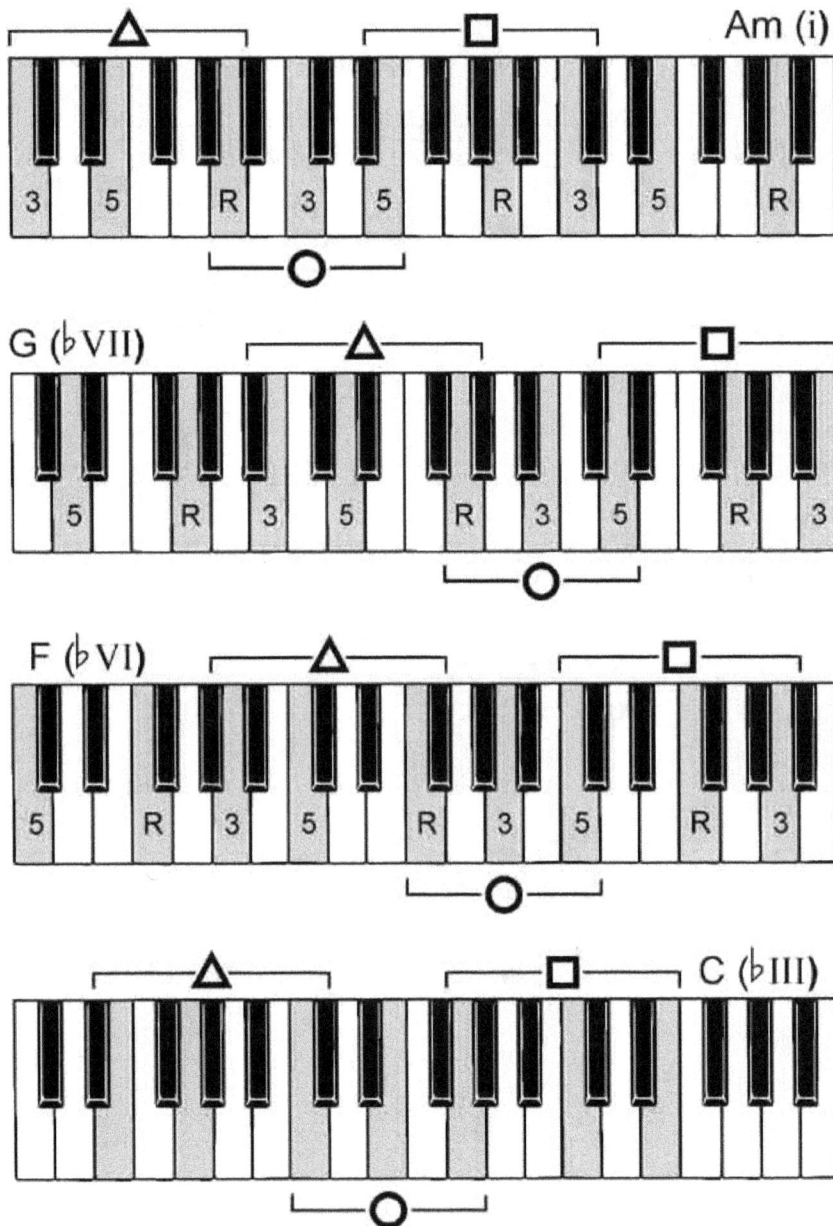

Here is the chord sequence. There's a four-bar introduction. Find the right hand chord inversions for the riff from the chord chart.

○ Am i	○ Am i	○ Am i	○ Am i	△ Am i	○ C ♭III	○ G ♭VII	○ C ♭III
△ Am i	○ C ♭III	○ G ♭VII	○ G ♭VII	△ Am i	○ C ♭III	○ G ♭VII	○ C ♭III
○ F ♭VI	○ G ♭VII	○ Am i	○ Am i	○ F ♭VI	○ G ♭VII	○ Am i	○ Am i

The chords in Roman numerals

Understanding the Roman numeral system of indicating chords moves your mastery of chords up a level. Try to find the chords using just this chart.

Key: A Aeolian							
○ i	○ i	○ i	○ i	△ i	○ ♭III	○ ♭VII	○ ♭III
△ i	○ ♭III	○ ♭VII	○ ♭VII	△ i	○ ♭III	○ ♭VII	○ ♭III
○ ♭VI	○ ♭VII	○ i	○ i	○ ♭VI	○ ♭VII	○ i	○ i

- The root of ♭III is three semitones (a minor third) above the tonic (A)
- The root of ♭VII is one whole tone (two semitones) below the tonic (A)
- The root of ♭VI is two whole tones (a major third) below the tonic (A)

Here (on the left) is the audio clip of just the chords, played through. You need to be able to play them at about this speed to proceed. On the right is the slightly simplified teaching version of the module riff. Find the chords and practice playing along with just one right hand chord per bar to start with. The chords written out are at the end of the module if you need them.

aeo_06_02   aeo_06_03

95

Stage Two: The melody

Try to pick up the melody from the riff audio, if you at all can. The chord chart will help you because melody notes are usually chord tones.

Picking out a melody by ear is the essence of the real musician's skill. You might find that you're better at this than you thought. In any event, practice is the way forward.

Here is the melody in MS. The introduction is not included.

aeo_06_04

The left hand in the audio clip (and the MIDI file) plays some quiet supporting triads you may wish to copy. The second half of the performance (second chorus) allows a little syncopation to creep in.

> NB: The module riff uses triplet ('swing') quavers. Written out triplet quavers make music look very confusing, so in popular music they are often just indicated by the marking at the right.

Stage Three: Playing both parts together

Now you try to 'meld' (to play together) the melody and the right hand chords in a three-four rhythm.

Study this annotated four-bar example.

1. The melody – treble clef, stems up, played by the little finger side of the right hand – takes first priority, always.

2. The rhythm chords – treble clef, stems down, played by the thumb side of the right hand – come on beats two and three of the bar, or just on beat two.

3. The left hand plays the root of the chord on beat one.

This is the teaching version of the module riff, repeated here for convenience. You are currently practising the right hand which you will be able to see clearly in the MidiPiano MIDI file performance.

aeo_06_03

Try your best to put together a performance from the chord sheet and melody MS, with the audio track for guidance. As a last resort, have a look at the written out music at the end of the module.

Learning the Musicarta way

1. Accurately written-out music of good, popular-styles keyboard performance is usually difficult for the popular music student to read. You therefore have to 'learn by doing'. This is where the Musicarta short-hands (counting, inversion symbols, BMT and TLR analysis) – plus, of course, the audio and MIDI clips – come into play. Pay attention to them – at least 50% as compared with 'the dots'. A performance built from these musical shorthands is much more valuable as a stepping stone to real creative keyboard musicianship than any number played from music.

2. You cannot 'learn by doing' without making mistakes. Unless you're a play-by-ear genius, you will not know every time exactly what that next piano key is going to sound like until you play it – though your guesswork can and will improve dramatically. So learn to use your mistakes to get better.

3. You might never need or want to play this riff as a solo performance – but you will be a really useful band member or jamming pal if you can keep up a steady but varied jazzy three-four texture. So settle happily for an intermediate stage – for the time being. You have to enjoy playing what you

97

are able to play, whatever that is. You should need a compelling reason to stop playing, not a compelling reason to start!

4. Learning to play the piano is a lot more like sports training than most musicians and teachers will admit. You practice tricks and textures like you would practice backhands, bunker shots, tumble turns, doubles on the dart board or whatever – ad nauseam. American jazz greats used to call this 'wood-shedding' – because family and friends would eventually drive them out to the wood shed to practice. Expect to do your share of 'wood shedding'–very few musicians become proficient without it.

Stage Four: Getting more syncopation into your playing

Listen again to the fully syncopated version of the module riff, and let's see how the plain three-four version is developed into this jazzy waltz texture.

aeo_06_01

For example, take the pattern we use for the introduction. (It could equally well be used to back your lead instrument or vocals.)

aeo_06_05

The only new development is the left hand quaver on "3 **and**".

Now syncopate the bass with a repeated note on "2 **and**":

aeo_06_06

98

Use the counting and the TLR (together, left, right) analysis to help you play along with the practice-speed audio.

Next thee right hand gets some syncopation. The first right hand chord is pulled forward into the "1 **and**" quaver slot.

aeo_06_07

When you can play that, practice it on two chords, A minor and G.

aeo_06_08

Now take the rhythm back one level to practise the separated melody on the little finger side of the right hand.

aeo_06_09

Now pull forward (again) the first right hand rhythm chords.

aeo_06_10

The developed bass line

The bass note on quaver count six is the perfect opportunity to introduce a 'moving note', where the bass part moves in an interesting way between the chord roots.

Moving note possibilities are:

1. A step-wise in-between note.
2. The note next door to the next root.
3. The fifth (chord tone) of the next chord.
4. No moving note at all.

Practice the bass line with just chords (no melody) in the right hand, as if you were just accompanying ('comping'). The numbered types of bass line movement are also shown in the following MS sketch.

If you were just comping, you would probably smooth out the top line of the right hand inversions as shown in the MS. For practice, work out these inversions and play them instead of the original chords.

aeo_06_11

These bass notes are the actual notes used in the jazzed-up version of the riff. Listen again and follow in the MS. You can practice at a much slower speed to start with, then start playing the right hand on beats two and three, then syncopated.

This is the end of the module material. Here are the full MS examples referred to earlier. These are the 'skeleton chords'.

aeo_06_02

Errata. Last chord of second line should read C. The inversion symbol is correct.

This is the full riff MS.

aeo_06_01

AEOLIAN FIVE-CHORD SET (PART 2)

This module adds iv ('Four minor') to the current Aeolian set – D minor in our A Aeolian key.

Get to know the module riff. | aeo_07_01 |

Here is the first part of the module riff, discussed below. | aeo_07_02 |

Finding the new chord

The D minor chord only appears in second inversion in this riff (square inversion symbol). Here is a recap of how you find any second inversion chord from its root position mother chord. (Read through even if you already know, for revision.)

Look at how the D minor right hand chord is written in the module riff MS. (These are the four chords you hear repeated at the start of the riff.)

- The top two notes are closest together. The bottom note is the note furthest away. Read from the bottom up, this is a P M M P M P chord.

- The two close-together notes are always from the simple root position (circle symbol) P M P M P chord. The top note of the root position chord has dropped down an octave to make the second inversion chord.

- Find a root position D minor chord – P M P M P, built on D. We are working in A Aeolian, an all-white-key mode, so you can safely just count off the white keys starting on D to find it. See it in your mind's eye, or work it out at the keyboard.

- Drop the top note (A) down an octave. You have your second inversion, square symbol, D minor chord. The root (name-note, D) is the middle note of a P M M P M P (second inversion) chord.

- Unless you see a 'slash chord' chord symbol, you can take it for granted that the left hand will be playing the root (D).

Work through all the opportunities presented to practice inverting triads. 'Seeing' the next inversion up or down of a chord makes playing interesting music much easier.

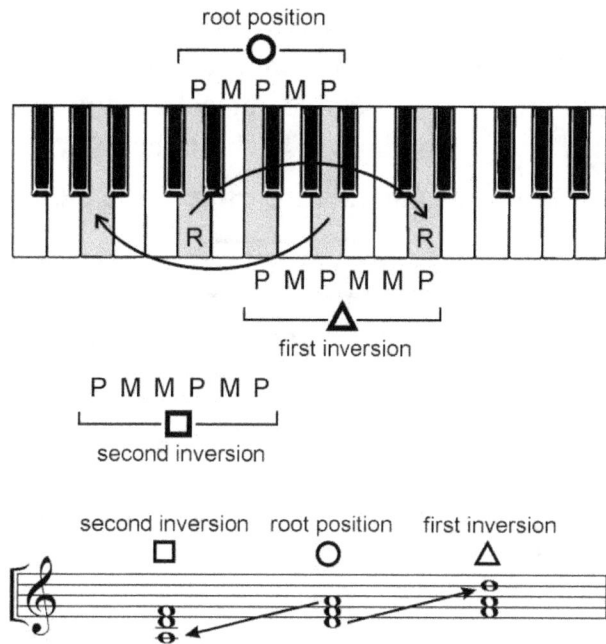

The module riff chords

Here are the skeleton chords for this module's riff.

aeo_07_03

i   v   iv   ♭VII   i   v   iv   ♭VII

i   v   iv   ♭VII   iv   v   ♭VI   ♭VII

105

Use the voice movement diagrams to help you learn the chords. Voice movement diagrams simply show on paper what the proficient pop musician is thinking: "The middle note stays the same, the two outside notes drop down…" "Everything goes down, perfectly parallel…", etc. Try to train yourself to think that way too.

Now we add some rhythm. Here is the pattern of the first six bars.

aeo_07_04

Tap out the beat map before tackling the notes.

aeo_07_BM1 (audio only)

This is the rhythm for the first six (3 x 2) bars. The D minor and G chords are dragged forward (anticipated). The BMT refers to the bottom, middle, top of the G chord.

If you have found your chords correctly, you should be able to play along with the first section audio for the six bars.

aeo_07_02

The last pair of bars has more syncopation and more BMT broken chord patterning.

aeo_07_BM2 (audio only)

Listen to this repeating audio/MIDI as you look at the beat map above. Work at it until you see what right hand notes to fill the pattern with and play the section.

aeo_07_05

That completes the first chorus of the module audio. In the second chorus, the bass part drops the plain minim rhythm and picks up the beat. The rhythms are all familiar from earlier modules in the series. Listen to the audio carefully, tap along, then 'tap' the chords and broken-chord chord tones at the keyboard in the rhythmic patterns you've identified. Expect to put in some hours getting a performance like this together!

A slow variation

Any chord sequence can be 'realised' (played) in an infinite number of ways. The middle section of the riff is a slower realisation of the first section chord sequence, in six-eight time.

aeo_07_06

This realisation uses two left hand accompaniment patterns. We used them before, in the Aeolian Four module. Recall how the two patterns are made out of the three chord tones of the root position triad.

Type One: R 5 8 10   **Type Two : 8 R 3 5**

We use two different patterns because the R 5 8 10 pattern down in E minor/D minor sounds too low.

In addition to the two patterns shown, we also need, for the accompaniment:

- A Type One G major pattern – the same shape as the A minor pattern but one key to the left;
- Another Type One pattern in F major, one key again to the left; and
- A Type Two D minor pattern – the same shape as the E minor pattern but shifted one key to the left.

Find these accompaniment patterns. Use this left-hand-only practice section to help you.

aeo_07_07

The MS for the slow section is on the next page. Study it as you listen to the audio again to see how it matches up. As usual, the melody is made up of chord tones on the beat with smoothing-out non-chord tones in between. All the notes on the MS are useful things to know about playing popular-styles keyboard.

aeo_07_06

The full module riff

The full module riff puts together the two sections you have learnt and finishes off by revisiting the faster first section material. Listen to the final section on its own (below) and build your performance from the audio clip and the following notes.

aeo_07_08

The 'reprise' (this final section) starts with both hands playing in the syncopated rhythm of the top line of the first beat map, with the left hand playing its chords an octave higher to keep the sound quite small.

aeo_07_BM1 (audio only)

Then the left hand drops and you play a fully syncopated chorus. To signal that the ending is approaching, you repeat the last four chords (D minor, E minor, F and G) twice, finishing with some strong A minor chords.

Train yourself to listen out for the structural features of songs and instrumental pop pieces like these. Knowing a piece's structure makes it easier to play – and remember. Learning about song form makes it easier to write songs or compose as well – you're not starting from scratch, you're filling a ready-made pattern with your own material.

MEDIANT SUBSTITUTION (PART 1)

Mediant substitution is a simple but powerful technique for making all your chord sequences sound more sophisticated. Listen to the riff we use to start our exploration.

med_01_01

The right hand in this riff plays only A minor and G chords, but mediant substitution makes the riff sound much more advanced.

Mediant substitution

Let's recap a i-♭VII (One minor/Flat Seven) modal minor pair – A minor and G.

med_01_02

Listen to what happens if, instead of playing the root of the G major chord in your left hand, you play the note a third down – E.

med_01_03

You can hear a more filled out sound. If we just played E minor chords (following the root in the left hand), we would have this.

med_01_04

Our mediant substitution 'slash chord' is definitely an improvement: we're getting the best of both worlds. Listen to it

med_01_03

again for comparison.

A 'slash chord' is a chord with a note that's not the chord root in the bass.

Writing down the mediant substitution chords

In the last MS (written-out music) example above you can see that our mediant substitution chord is indicated using two different chord symbols:

1. As a slash chord – "G over E".; and
2. As Em7 (E minor seven)

The first chord symbol – slash chord G over E – describes what the chord looks like and how you can easily make it: you play a G major triad in the right hand and the note E in the bass. We will use this formula to make lots of great-sounding seventh chords

The second chord symbol – Em7 (E minor seven) – is the 'proper' name for the chord. Seventh cords are four-note chords

Substituting another pair of inversions

Let's use the same mediant substitution process on another pair of A minor and G inversions. Play the chords 'straight' first.

med_01_05

Now, shift the bass down a third (mediant substitution) for both chords.

med_01_06

You see here another way of writing slash chords here. They are still called "A minor over F" and "G over E", but the bass note is written after a slash and not underneath it.

In the second half of the MS, you see the proper names of the chords: "F major 7" and "E minor 7". Notice the alternative way of writing the E minor 7 chord symbol – Emin7 instead of Em7. You will find both versions in pop sheet music.

Minor and major seventh chords

A seventh chord is a four-note chord. In its simplest form, it is a root position triad (root, third, fifth) with another note a third above the fifth – the seventh note counting up the scale from the root.

Here are our two seventh chords – F major 7 and E minor 7 – in root position.

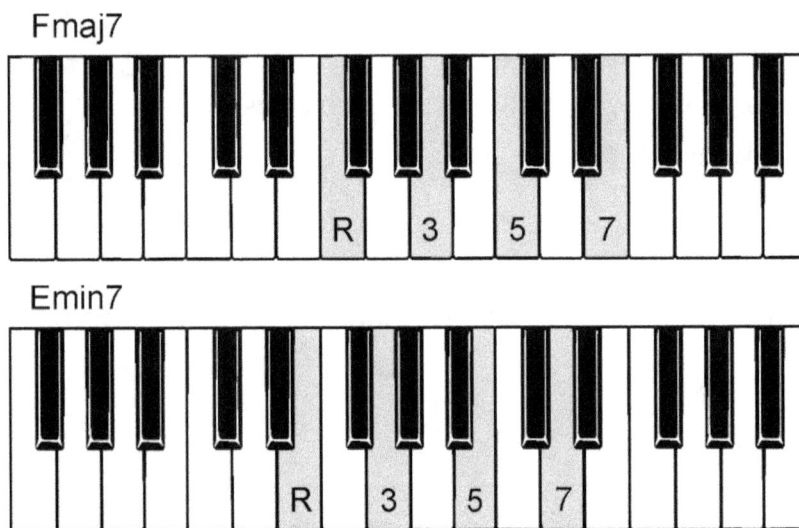

Fmaj7

Emin7

In all-white-key A Aeolian, you can form these seventh chords (in root position) by playing the root, missing a key, playing one and so on until you have four notes.

There are four varieties of seventh chord. For a full explanation and an essential keyboard drill for learning the five types, visit Musicarta's Seventh Chords page.

Making seventh chords with mediant substitution

We have discovered that A MINOR SEVENTH CHORD looks like

The **root** plus a **major chord** built on the note **a minor third higher**

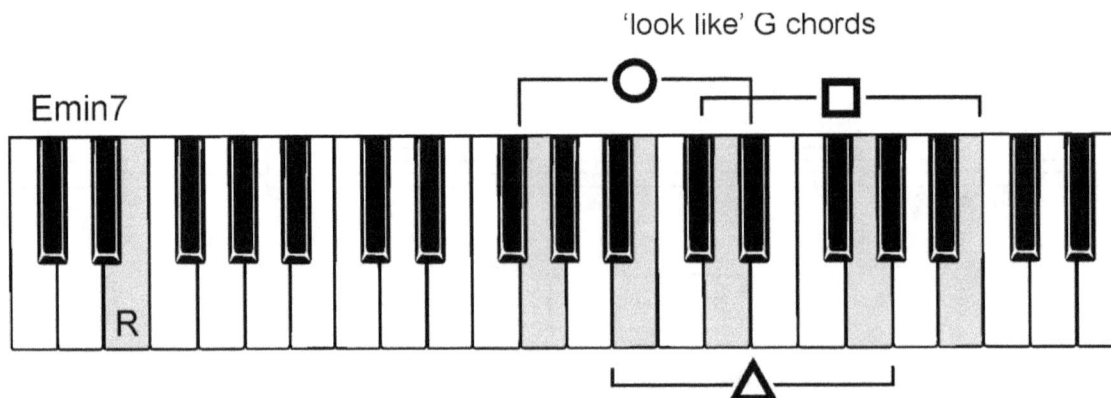

'look like' G chords

Emin7

Any of the G inversions over an E will make and E minor 7 chord. Play the root in the left hand and any three-note inversion in the right.

A MAJOR SEVENTH CHORD looks like

The root plus a minor chord built on the note a major third higher

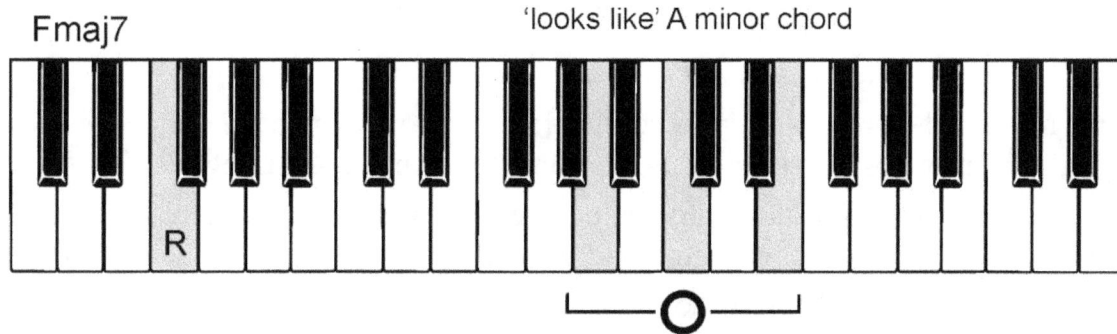

Fmaj7

'looks like' A minor chord

R

Any A minor inversion over the F would make an F major 7 chord. The keyboard shows only the F major 7 chord in this module's riff. Invert the A minor chord to make other Fmaj7 chords.

Trying out mediant substitution chords

Mediant substitution chords are chords you 'try out'. They will nearly always harmonise your existing melody in an interesting, even improved, way.

Mediant substitution is a simple process with a fancy name. You create mediant substitution chords – to try them out – by dropping the root of the existing chord a third.

You drop the root of a **major chord** a **minor third** (three semitones) to get a substitute minor seventh chord on the new root.

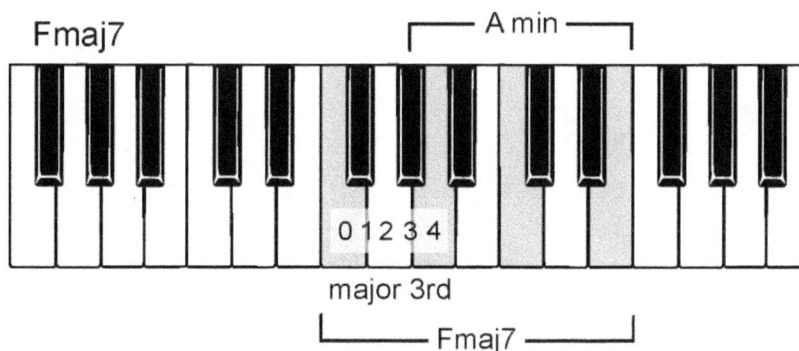

Fmaj7

A min

0 1 2 3 4

major 3rd

Fmaj7

You drop the root of a **minor chord** a **major third** (four semitones) to get a substitute major seventh chord on the new root.

113

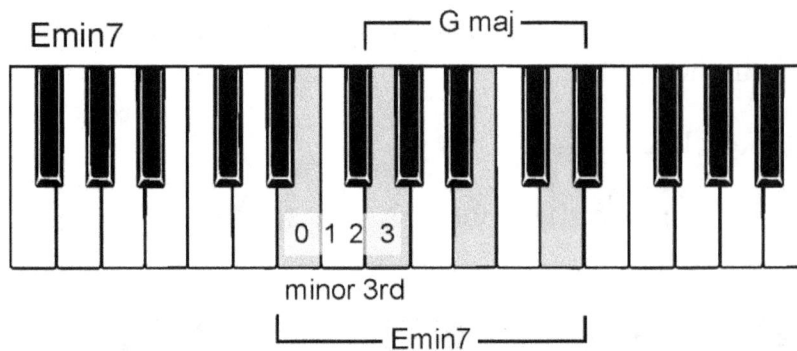

To use this method shown in the keyboard illustrations above, you need to make sure you are working with the root position triad of the chord that you are substituting.

After that, the new root will usually drop an octave or two into the left hand, and the right hand will play whatever inversion of the triad the melody/top note makes necessary.

These mediant substitution seventh chords make the modal chord sequences sound a lot more sophisticated. In the next module, we practice the process on other i-♭VII (One Minor/Flat Seven) chord pairs. Dropping seventh chords into chord sequences will soon become second

MEDIANT SUBSTITUTION (PART 2)

Mediant substitution is a simple but powerful technique for making all your chord sequences sound more sophisticated. This module applies the mediant substitution technique to the three modal minor i-♭VII riffs in Minor Modes (2).

The left hand column in the table below gives the reference for the original version. The right-hand column showcases the same three riffs treated with mediant substitution.

Original	Treated with mediant substitution
min_02_04	med_02_01
min_02_05	med_02_02
min_02_06	med_02_03

In this module, you practice the mediant substitution process and experiment with the new sounds you can create from simple two-chord material.

The first riff

Here is the first riff in the table above, original and treated.

min_02_04	med_02_01

Revise the original riff. Here are the right hand i-♭VII inversions used and the chord sequence.

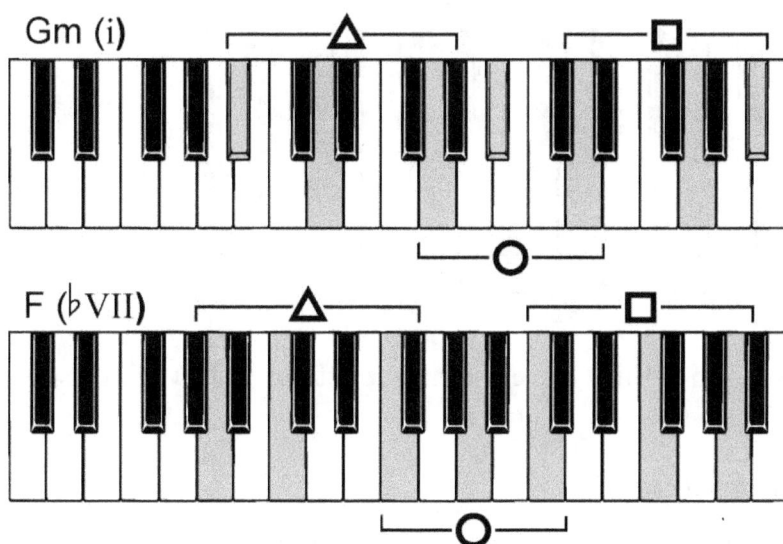

△	△	O	O	△	△	O	O
Gm	: F	Gm	: F	Gm	: F	Gm	: F

△	△	O	O	□	□	△	△
Gm	: F	Gm	: F	Gm	: F	Gm	: F

Making the mediant substitution chords

This is how to make the mediant substitute seventh chord for G minor.

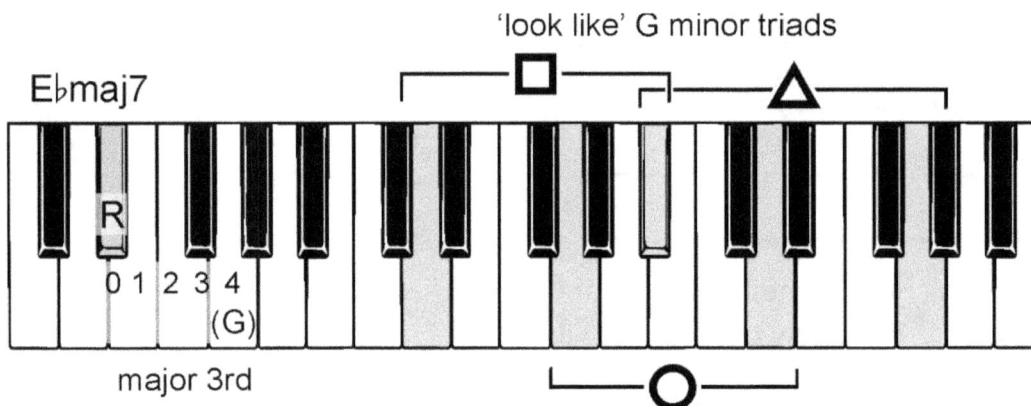

You lower the root of the G minor chords a major third (two whole tones, four semitones) to create E flat major seventh chords.

This is how to make the mediant substitute seventh chord for the F chords.

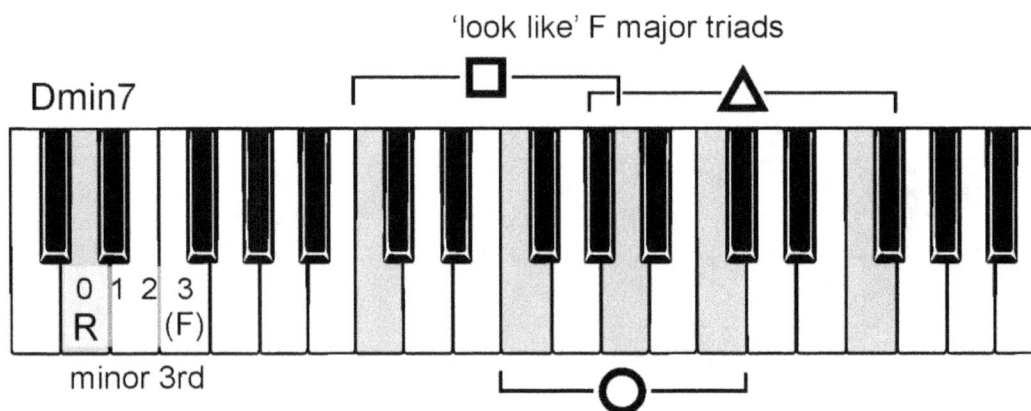

You lower the root of the F chords a minor third (three semitones) to create D minor seventh chords.

The mediant substitution chord sequences

Here is the chord sequence of the riff treated with mediant substitution, shown as slash chords. (There is no change in the first line.)

△ Gm : △ F	○ Gm : ○ F	△ Gm : △ F	○ Gm : ○ F
△ Gm/E♭ : △ F/D	○ Gm/E♭ : ○ F	□ Gm/E♭ : □ F/D	△ Gm/E♭ : △ F

However, it is not usual to write seventh chords as slash chords. (This is a Musicarta 'starter' technique for looking at and learning them.) Here is the chord sequence written out using conventional chord symbols.

△ Gm : △ F	○ Gm : ○ F	△ Gm : △ F	○ Gm : ○ F
E♭maj7 : Dmin7	E♭maj7 : F	E♭maj7 : Dmin7	E♭maj7 : F

Note that we cannot use the circle/square/triangle method to indicate seventh chord inversions.

Use the keyboard diagrams and the chord sequence charts to play the mediant substitution version of the first riff.

| med_02_01 |

The second riff

Here are the original and treated versions of the second Minor Modes (2) riff.

| min_02_05 | med_02_02 |

The second riff uses chords E minor and D major. Revise the original riff.
Here is the original riff chord sequence.

△ Em	△ D	○ Em	○ D	□ Em	□ D	△ Em	△ D
△ Em	△ D	○ Em	○ D	□ Em	□ D	△ Em	△ D

Here are the mediant substitution chords for E minor and D.

117

'look like' E minor triads

Cmaj7

0 1 2 3 4
R   (E)
major 3rd

'look like' D major triads

Bmin7

0 1 2 3
R   (D)
minor 3rd

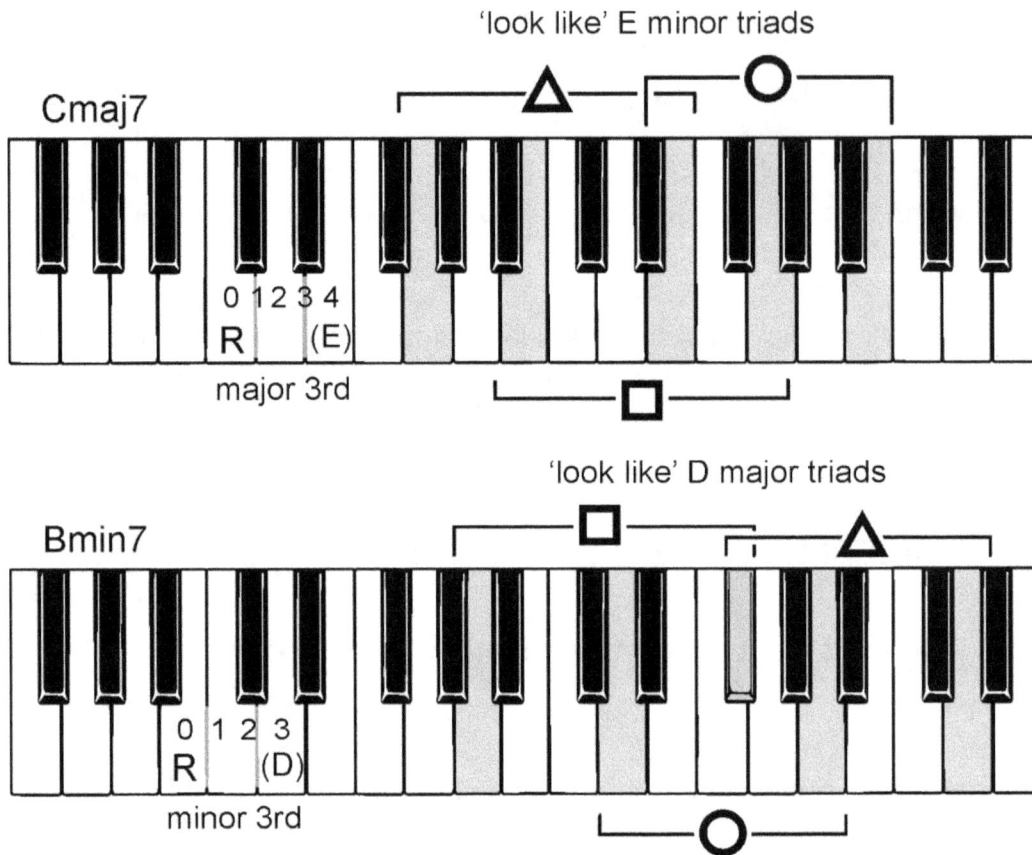

Three possible mediant substitution variations

You, the improviser/composer, choose when and where to use mediant substitution to vary your chord sequences.

Here are three possible mediant substitute versions of the second Minor Modes (2) riff.

Here is a version with substitutions in the second half of the line.

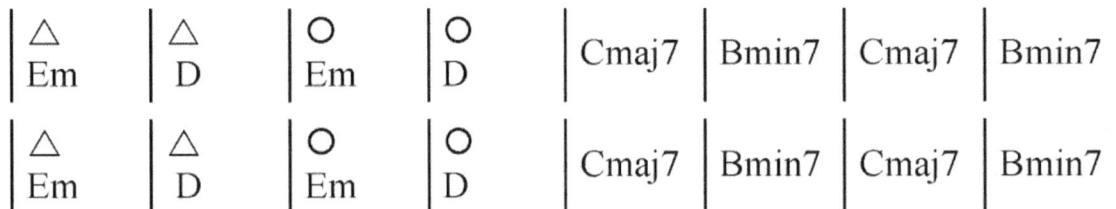

| △ Em | △ D | ○ Em | ○ D | Cmaj7 | Bmin7 | Cmaj7 | Bmin7 |
| △ Em | △ D | ○ Em | ○ D | Cmaj7 | Bmin7 | Cmaj7 | Bmin7 |

med_02_02

You might introduce substitutions earlier in the line and climb back out at the end:

Em	D		Cmaj7	Bmin7	Cmaj7	Bmin7	Cmaj7	D	

Em	D		Cmaj7	Bmin7	Cmaj7	Bmin7	Cmaj7	D	

| med_02_04 |

The extreme is to have substitution all the way through.

Cmaj7	Bmin7	Cmaj7	Bmin7	Cmaj7	Bmin7	Cmaj7	Bmin7	

Cmaj7	Bmin7	Cmaj7	Bmin7	Cmaj7	Bmin7	Cmaj7	D	

| med_02_05 |

The last chord has been left as D major, but notice how the sequence still wants to cadence into E minor – the mode has got into your head!

Play and listen to the three versions. Think about why and when one version might be preferable to the others. Make your own variation and write it down. You can use slash chords for notation if you prefer.

> *Errata.* Last line of above audio is Em / Bm7 repeating.

The third Minor Modes riff

The third Minor Modes (2) riff uses D minor and C major chords. Revise the original riff, and compare the original and mediant substitution versions.

| min_02_06 | med_02_03 |

Here are the keyboards showing the D minor and C mediant substitution chords you will be using.

'look like' D minor triads

Bbmaj7

R
0 1 2 3 4
(D)
major 3rd

'look like' C major triads

Amin7

0 1 2 3
R (C)
minor 3rd

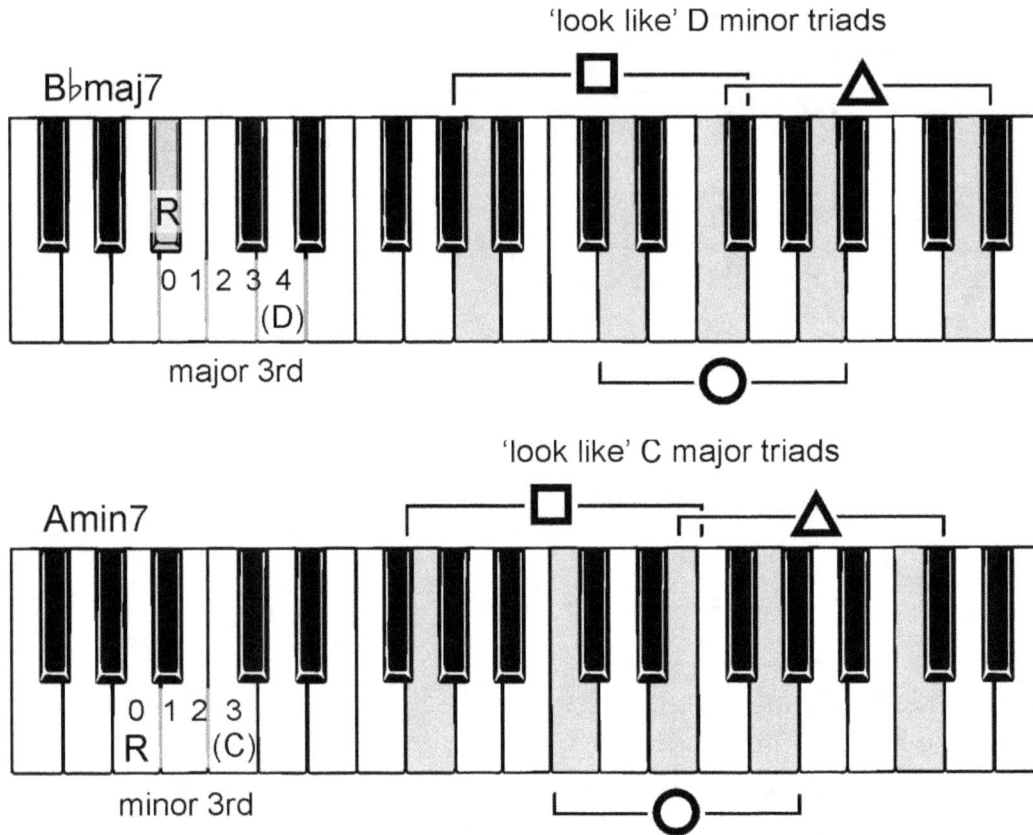

The original chord sequence is:

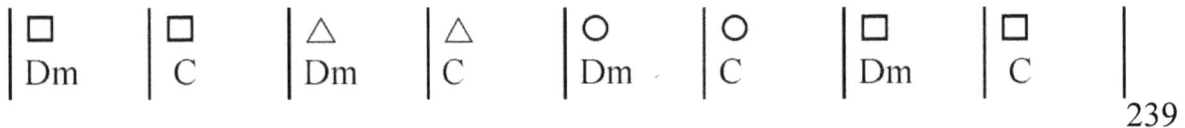

□	□	△	△	○	○	□	□
Dm	C	Dm	C	Dm	C	Dm	C

239

A chord sequence using all the possible mediant substitutions would be:

Bbmaj7	Amin7	Bbmaj7	Amin7	Bbmaj7	Amin7	Bbmaj7	Amin7

240

Listen to the audio of the treated version. Try to hear what substitutions have been made. Make a note – any shorthand will do – and play what you have written down.

med_02_03

MEDIANT SUBSTITUTION (PART 3)

This module applies the mediant substitution technique to the i-♭VII-♭VI chord sequence (One minor, Flat Seven and Flat Six) from the Aeolian One module.

In A Aeolian minor, these chords are A minor (i), G (♭VII) and F (♭VI) – three all-white-key chords. Run through the three sets of inversions of the three chords.

med_03_01

Making a practice piece

med_03_02

You can make practising the inversions sound more musical by using the G chord from the next set of inversions to transition between positions (circled in the following MS example), and finishing it off neatly.

Practising cycling through the three sets of inversions in a chord sequence like this will put chords under your fingertips faster than anything else.

Add a beat and a broken chord pattern, and you're learning something usable as you practice. The BMT (bottom, middle, top) pattern used for the first six bars is: 252

```
T B M T   T M B       T B M T   T M B
Am :  G           F  :  G
```

(The colon **:** indicates that the bar is split equally between the two chords.)

The second time the chord sequence is played, the first note of the second (and fourth and sixth) bar is dragged forward (anticipated). Listen carefully to the audio clip until you can hear it, and imitate it – once you can play the 'straight' version.

Creating a riff with mediant substitution chords

Mediant substitution is a way of making your chords sound richer by lowering the root of the existing three-note chords (triads) to create new seventh chords.

If we shift the bass line of the last music sample down a third (except for the last two chords), we get this.

med_03_03

This audio demonstration of mediant substitution plays through the substituted seventh chords twice, then adds broken chord and rhythmic variation to turn the exercise into a usable riff.

Here is the written out music for the riff performance.

The BMT analysis (bottom, middle, top, plus C for chord) refers the 'looks like' triads played as the upper part of the seventh chords. Refer to the keyboards diagrams earlier if necessary to remind yourself what these are.

Students of solo keyboard style will find close study of the fingering given here rewarding. There are very few alternatives if you want to play both chords and melody in your right hand – as a solo performer must. Use solo pieces like this as exercises to make your hand learn the necessary skills and conform to the requirements of the style.

Mixed original and mediant substitution chords

The audio riff above uses all the possible mediant substitution seventh chords. The ear can find this overwhelming. Here are some riffs which mix original chords and mediant substitution seventh chords.

Mixed Riff 1

The right hand still plays only A minor, G and F triads. The bass (left hand) is either dropped a third to create mediant substitution seventh chords or not. Seventh chords are written 'properly', not as slash chords. Work out from the keyboards above which 'looks like' triad to play.

The right hand chords are shown stems-down. Find these first, as in the audio file.

med_03_04

The stems-up notes are the melody, which you will add once you know the chords. You have to finger the chords so that you don't run out of fingers for the melody. Drop the rhythm while you drill the melody.

med_03_05

Last, add the rhythm. You don't have to play exactly what's in the audio clip – any jazzed-up version will do.

med_03_06

Mixed riff 2

med_03_07

The audio plays the chords straight (with the 'repeat three times'), then with syncopated right hand chords and straight bass, then with the bass joining in the syncopation. Sing or clap along with the syncopated part to get the rhythm.

The right hand is still playing just A minor, G and F triads. Look at the shape of them – they are all first inversion P M P M M P triads (triangle symbol). Exactly half of them are mediant substitution seventh chords.

This riff goes well with the previous riff, and would work as a backing for a solo or vocal.

Create your own 'mixed' type riff

Revisit this Aeolian One module riff and see how much mediant substitution (dropping the bass a third) you think it needs.

Here are the chords and the full riff audio.

aeo_01_05

Revisit the relevant part of Aeolian One module to build up the rhythmic/broken chord texture if necessary.

125

Here are the chords with the bass line dropped a third (all mediant substitution).

med_03_08

Here's how to proceed.

- Play the original riff right hand texture over the new mediant substitution bass line to hear what it sounds like.

- Play the original again.

- Decide where you would drop the bass to get the mediant substitution seventh chords and where you would leave it as it is. Remember that you can repeat the riff, so you can make more than one choice.

- Write down the chord sequence of the mix you decide is best.

- Try joining the result up with the two riffs in this module to make an extended riff.

Every time you apply the mediant substitution process to a set of chords you deepen your understanding of how the harmony of popular music works. More and more chords will seem to 'just appear' under your fingertips.

MEDIANT SUBSTITUTION (PART 4)

This module applies the mediant substitution technique to the Aeolian four-chord set in D Aeolian minor

Aeolian minor	i 'One minor'	♭VII 'Flat Seven'	♭VI 'Flat Six'	v 'Five minor'
D	D minor	C	B♭	A minor
A	A minor	G	F	E minor
G	G minor	F	E♭	D minor
E	E minor	D	C	B minor

In D Aeolian minor, the chords are D minor, C, B♭ and A minor. The other sets of chords in the table above are there to help you use the Roman numeral system to understand and transpose this group of chords – and others.

Here are all the inversions of the module chords shown on keyboards. Run through them using any broken chord pattern of your choosing.

Here's a riff on these four chords with no mediant substitution at all.

> med_04_01

This is the chord sequence.

The right hand chords are shown as triads with inversion symbols. Find them using the keyboard diagrams. Here's a slow audio performance of the riff skeleton chords.

> med_04_02

Here is an MS sketch of the riff chords with the broken chord BMT analysis.

Look out for the anticipation. All the C-for-chords in the BMT analysis are the next chord, anticipated (pulled forward a quaver).

The right hand strays a long way down into the between-the-staves leger lines. Here is the right hand written an octave higher but with the *8vb* (play an octave lower) sign. Use it if it helps.

When you can find the chords without any trouble, study the BMT analysis as you listen, and copy the audio. Here it is again.

$$\boxed{\text{med\_04\_01}}$$

The riff with mediant substitution

Now start treating some of the chords with mediant substitution. You drop the bass note a third down the D Aeolian minor scale from the root of the chord. Here's a quick reference table.

Original root (chord):	Dm	C	B♭	A
Mediant substitution root:	B♭	A	G	F

Here's one possibility.

□	○	□	△	□	△	□	□	□
Dm	: Am	B♭	: C	B♭/G	: C/A	B♭/G	: B♭/C C	

The right hand chords are still shown as triads with inversion symbols and the mediant substitution seventh chords are shown as slash chords. (There is one slash chord – B♭/C in the last bar – which is not a mediant substitution chord.)

Here is a practice-speed audio performance of the chords on the left and a possible performance on the right.

$$\boxed{\text{med\_04\_03}}\ \boxed{\text{med\_04\_04}}$$

Except for the last half-bar, all the chords in the second half have been substituted (the root has been lowered a third).

Now apply mediant substitution everywhere you can.

□	○	□	△	□	△	□	□	△
Dm/B♭	Am/F	B♭/G	C/A	B♭/G	C/A	B♭/G	B♭/C	C

Written in proper seventh chords, that sequence is:

B♭maj7   Fmaj7   Gmin7   Amin7   Gmin7   Amin7   Gmin7   B♭/C :C

Here is the 'skeleton chord' performance, plus a gentle broken-chord 'realisation' of the sequence.

$$\boxed{\text{med\_04\_05}}\ \boxed{\text{med\_04\_06}}$$

Remind yourself of the mediant substitution process.

Your right hand triads stay the same but…

…you lower the root a third to make mediant substitution seventh chords.

The best-sounding chord sequences are a mix of the original chords, some mediant substitution chords and some 'reverse mediant substitution' chords – explained in the following section.

Reverse mediant substitution

Mediant substitution works because chords a third apart share two chord tones (and the other chord tone creates an interesting seventh chord.)

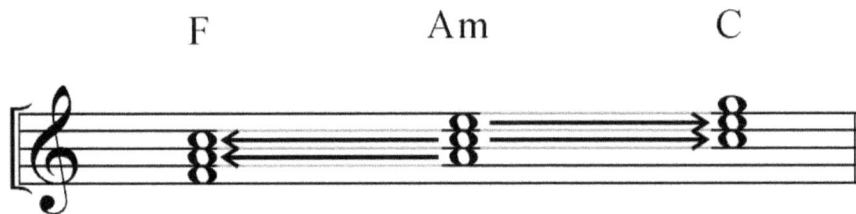

The common chord tones

Mediant substitution works both ways. You can either lower the root a third to get a seventh chord on the new root (ordinary mediant substitution), or raise the whole triad a third to get a seventh chord on the existing root (reverse mediant substitution).

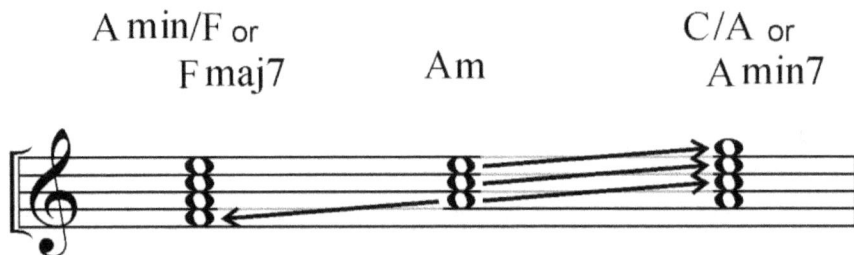

Ordinary mediant substitution - add a new root a third lower.

Reverse mediant substitution - raise the whole triad a third.

The only usable new chord reverse substitution gives when applied to our four chords is D minor 7.(see below), but reverse substitution lets us use our existing mediant substitution seventh chords in more places – as discussed in the following section.

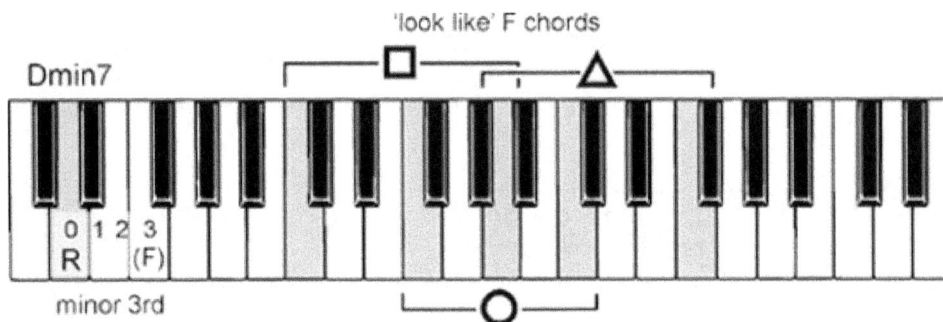

Alternative mediant substitution chord harmonies

Mediant substitution shows us that we can use any of the chords in the following table under the riff's four top notes. (Proper spellings for the mediant substitution seventh chords are given in brackets.)

Original chord	□ Dm	○ Am	□ B♭	△ C
Ordinary med. subs. chords	□ Dm/B♭ (= B♭maj7)	○ Am/F (= Fmaj7)	□ B♭/G (= Gmin7)	△ C/A (= Amin7)
Reverse med. subs. chords	△ F/D (= Dmin7)	□ C/A (= Amin7)	△ Dm/B♭ (= B♭maj7)	□ Am/F (= Fmaj7)

Here are some sample chord sequences using chords from the table above. From now on, proper spellings for the mediant substitution seventh chords are used, and the 'slash chord' spellings are in brackets.

Dm7 : Am7	B♭maj7: Am7	B♭maj7: Amin7	Gmin7 : B♭/C C
(F/D) (C/A)	(Dm/B♭) (C/A)	(Dm/B♭) (C/A)	(B♭/G)

med_04_07	med_04_08

B♭maj7: Am7	B♭maj7: Fmaj7	Gmin7 : Amin7	Gmin7 : B♭/C C
(Dm/B♭) (C/A)	(Dm/B♭) (Am/F)	(B♭/G) (C/A)	(B♭/G)

med_04_09	med_04_10

Dm : Am7	Gmin7 : Fmaj7	B♭maj7: Fmaj7	Gmin7 : B♭/C C
(C/A)	(B♭/G) (Am/F)	(Dm/B♭) (Am/F)	(B♭/G)

med_04_11	med_04_12

B♭maj7: Fmaj7	Gmin7 : Am7	Gmin7 : Fmaj7	Gmin7 : B♭/C C
(Dm/B♭) (Am/F)	(B♭/G) (C/A)	(B♭/G) (Am/F)	(B♭/G)

med_04_13	med_04_14

Putting together your own chord sequence

When you can substitute chords like this – potentially three for every melody note – you have multiple choices. Lining up all the chord sequences for the module riff vertically (below), you can in theory jump to any chord in the next column.

Here's what putting together a chord sequence from all the options might look like on paper.

f e	d c	d c	d d c
Dm : Am	Bb : C	Bb : C	Bb : Bb/C C
Dm : Am	Bb : C	Gmin7 : Amin7 (Bb/G) (C/A)	Gmin7 : Bb/C C (Bb/G)
Dm7 : Am7 (F/D) (C/A)	Bbmaj7 : Am7 (Dm/Bb) (C/A)	Bbmaj7 : Am7 (Dm/Bb) (C/A)	Gmin7 : Bb/C C (Bb/G)
Bbmaj7 : Am7 (Dm/Bb) (C/A)	Bbmaj7 : Fmaj7 (Dm/Bb) (Am/F)	Gmin7 : Am7 (Bb/G) (C/A)	Gmin7 : Bb/C C (Bb/G)
Dm : Am7 (C/A)	Gmin7 : Fmaj7 (Bb/G) (Am/F)	Bbmaj7 : Fmaj7 (Dm/Bb) (Am/F)	Gmin7 : Bb/C C (Bb/G)
Bbmaj7 : Fmaj7 (Dm/Bb) (Am/F)	Gmin7 : Am7 (Bb/G) (C/A)	Gmin7 : Fmaj7 (Bb/G) (Am/F)	Gmin7 : Bb/C C (Bb/G)

The first chord sequence – the original – has the top notes of the right hand chords above the chord symbols, to remind you. Proper spellings for the mediant substitution seventh chords are used, but the 'slash chord' spellings are given in brackets to help you construct the chords on the fly.

Play the two chord sequences indicated. Here are audios of just the simple chords – make a performance in the style of the module. The sequence starting on D minor comes first.

med_04_15	med_04_16

Try out the possible mediant substitution basses and write down the versions you like most in the table on the next page.

Original chord	☐ Dm	○ Am	☐ B♭	△ C	☐ B♭	△ C	☐ B♭	☐ B♭	: ☐ B♭ ☐ C
Ordinary med. subs. chords	B♭maj7 ☐ Dm/B♭	Fmaj7 ○ Am/F	Gmin7 ☐ B♭/G	Amin7 △ C/A	Gmin7 ☐ B♭/G	Amin7 △ C/A	Gmin7 ☐ B♭/G	Gm7 ☐ B♭/G	
Reverse med. subs. chords	Dmin7 △ F/D	Amin7 ☐ C/A	B♭maj7 △ Dm/B♭		B♭maj7 △ Dm/B♭		B♭maj7 △ Dm/B♭		
Reharmonised chords		☐ C		Fmaj7 ☐ Am/F		Fmaj7 ☐ Am/F			
Your chord sequences									

THE DORIAN MODE

The Dorian mode occurs naturally on the white keys from D to D ("D for Dorian").

| DORIAN | white keys from D to D | minor seventh scale |

W S W W W S W

The Dorian mode uses the key signature of the key one whole tone below.

Like the Aeolian, the Dorian is a minor mode. The difference lies in the sixth degree (note) of the scale, which gives the Dorian mode a major subdominant chord, IV.

	i	ii	♭III	IV	v		♭VII
Dorian	minor	minor	major	major	minor		major
Aeolian	i		♭III	iv	v	♭VI	♭VII
	minor		major	minor	minor	major	major

(As usual in the comparison tables, the diminished triad is stripped out.)

Dorian Riff – Modes Diary 24-06-14

The major subdominant chord creates a signature Dorian pair, i–IV, familiar from the blues and jazz-funk which the module riff showcases. Listen to it a few times to let the tonality 'sink in'. The full MS is at the end of the module.

dor_01_01

Here's the signature Dorian i–IV pair in all its inversions. The MS has the classical D minor key signature – B♭ – so there are B naturals throughout (which tells you the music is modal). The second pass-through in the audio/MIDI clips has a pedal D bass with a little rhythm added.

dor_01_02

Without the major IV chord, that music would sound like the clip, below left. (This is also what the classical minor key would offer – use the same MS but ignore the B natural (♮) signs.). Compare with the major IV version (below right) to fully appreciate the modal tonality.

dor_01_03   dor_01_02

The riff itself uses plenty of reverse mediant substitution in the right hand – that is, third-up F chords, creating D minor 7 chords. Here is the inversions drill incorporating Dmin7 chords.

dor_01_04

Here is a repeating audio/MIDI clip of just the first section of the module riff, which is built exclusively on D minor or minor 7 (i, i7) and G major (IV) chords. Use it as a play along track to practice your inversions.

dor_01_05

135

Dorian harmony

Modes excel in providing strings of chords where the root falls a fourth. We have already come across the Mixolydian version – here in C.

dor_01_06

The Dorian mode provides a four-chord cascade down to the home chord.

dor_01_07

You hear the skeleton chords segue into the second part of the module riff.

These four chords sound particularly nice because the chords are:

major (♭III – F), major (♭VII – C), major (IV – G), minor (i – D minor)

If you play the same sequence in the Aeolian mode, the minor subdominant will give you F–C–G minor–D minor – still useable, but much 'darker'.

dor_01_08

Use the MS above, ignoring the B naturals, to get the Aeolian version. In the second part of the audio, the right hand cycles through another set of F–C–Gm–Dm inversions with a bass line variation – see if you can 'play it by ear', or just copy the MIDI.

Syncopation in the module riff

Here is the riff chord sequence.

'Verse'

Dm7	:G	Dm7	Dm	Dm7	:G	Dm7	Dm

'Chorus'

F	C	G	Dm	F	C	G	Dm7

:G	Dm7	Dm

Notice the odd phrase length – the eleven-bar 'Chorus'. Music usually comes in multiples of four bars, and slight variations on the pattern like this help make music interesting – although most listeners would not know what it was exactly about the piece that made it so.

The rocking-octave bass

The rocking-octave bass is quite hard work but worth it for any rock-styles keyboard player. The first eight bars of the MS show a simplified practice-only version using just crotchets which doesn't actually occur anywhere in the recorded performance.

dor_01_09

That by itself is an acceptable 'stepping stone' performance! Next, practice quavers in the left hand, or perhaps a mix, as here. (This is what the left hand does in the chorus.)

dor_01_10

137

The next development would be the 'flapping thumb' (with the held little finger).

dor_01_11

The thumb need not play every 'flap', nor the little finger always hold for a full bar.

In practice, once you have mastered a number of varieties, your left hand will (should) vary itself according to what the right hand is playing. Watch the module riff MIDI performance on MidiPiano to pick up particular patterns to practice. (It's useful to study screen-shots to clarify what's actually happening.)

The right hand

In the 'Verse', the melody actually plays inside the right hand chord.

dor_01_12

A screen-shot of this material in MidiPiano Piano Roll view makes it clear what you're asking your fingers to do.

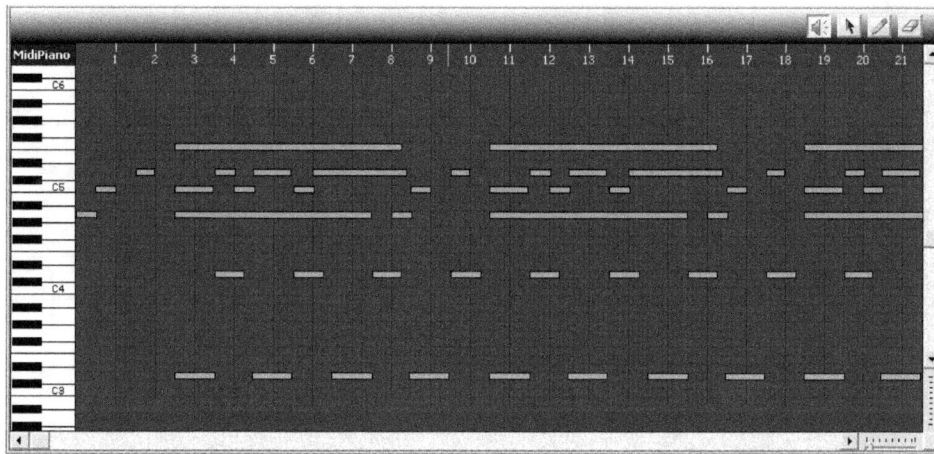

In the Chorus section, the right hand has its own version of thumb-side 'flapping'. Here is an exercise for the essentials of the technique.

dor_01_13

Get the right hand going first. A simpler left hand would be quite acceptable to practice over. – the 'flapping thumb' would be best.

When you can play that, start introducing some syncopation in the top line – in particular, anticipation over the bar line.

Remember, your goal is to develop keyboard skills and get a 'keep going' performance out there, not to simply reproduce another performance. You build truly creative keyboard musicianship by building on 'what you could do the time before' – not on what you wish you could do, if only…!

The Musicarta Modes Workbook is also about knowing how the modes in particular can be used to put music together, and give you a starting point for your own compositions.

Dorian Riff - Modes Diary 24-06-14

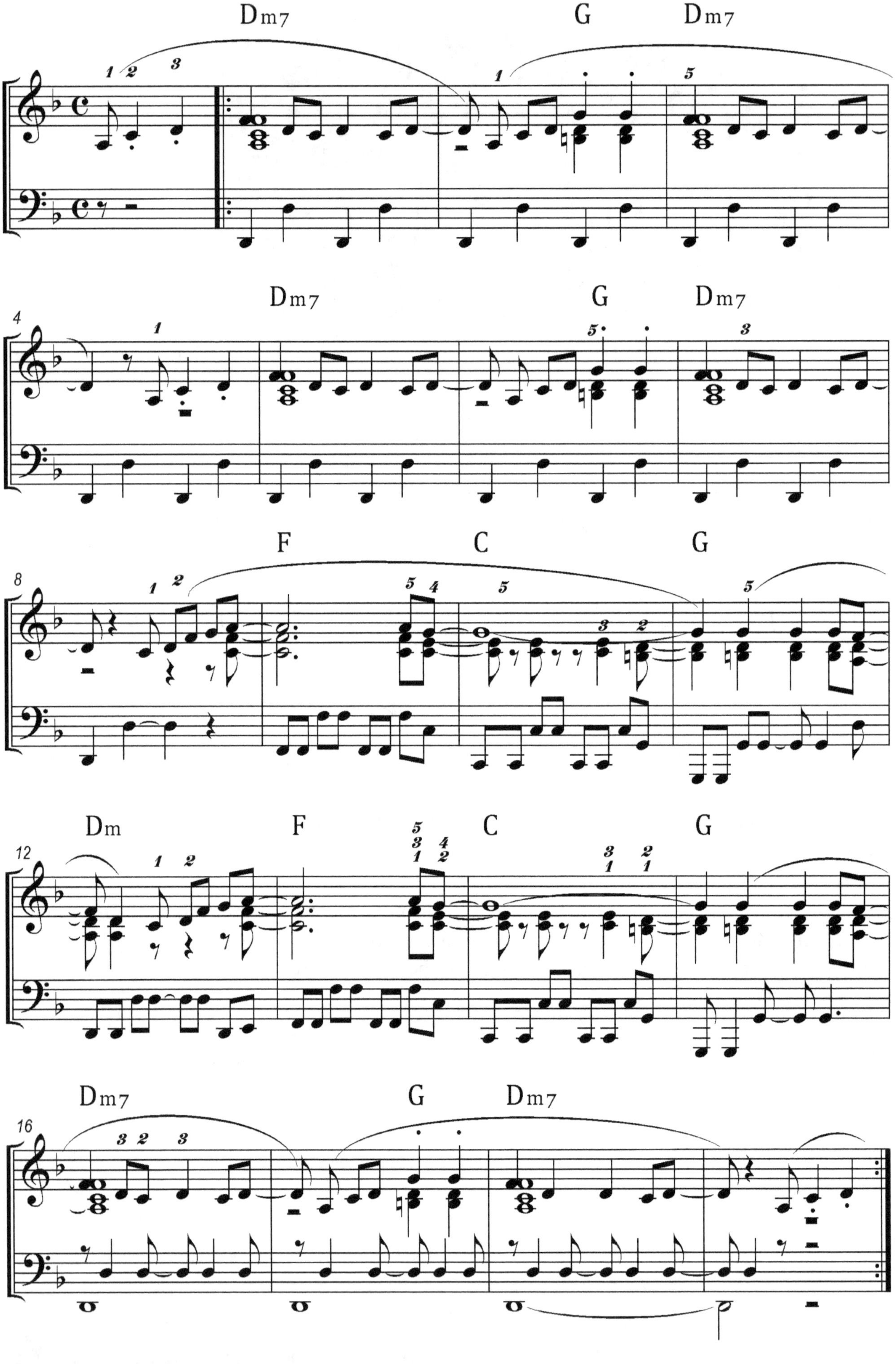

THE SPANISH SKETCHES

Spanish flamenco music uses a familiar variant of the four-chord Aeolian set. Listen to this module's performance, 'Spanish Sketches'.

> sup_spa_01

You may remember at the start of our Aeolian explorations, we said that 'v' ('five minor') doesn't make a very good cadence with 'i' ('one minor'). 'V' ('five major') is a much better cadencing chord.

Listen to this audio example. You will hear i, v, i (E minor, B minor, E minor) followed by i, V, i (E minor, B major, E minor), in the three pairs of closest inversions. See if you can play the chord changes just from the audio.

> sup_spa_02

The typically Spanish chord sequence explored in this module takes the best of both worlds. It uses both the Aeolian ♭VII chord and the major dominant, 'V', which would not normally occur together in either conventional minor keys or modes proper.

This 'Spanish changes' group of chords consists of i, ♭VII, ♭VI and V. Here they are, in four keys.

The 'Spanish changes'			
i (key) 'one minor'	♭VII 'flat seven'	♭VI 'flat six'	V 'five'
E minor	D	C	B
A minor	G	F	E
D minor	C	B♭	A
G minor	F	E♭	D

The Spanish changes in E minor

We are going to explore this chord sequence in E minor. Our familiar white-key A Aeolian minor goes too low for this music. (Note that this is a powerful reason for using the Roman numeral system to help you transpose – some music just sounds better higher up or lower down.)

See the Spanish changes chords on the familiar keyboards, below. Run through the inversions.

The new B chord is quite challenging. It's mainly on the black notes, which means that your hand needs to be well up the keys to play it. This can feel sometimes feel wrong at first, but in fact it's a good habit to cultivate because it puts the black keys within easy reach.

Check your knowledge of the B major inversions especially using the Musicarta Inversions drill.

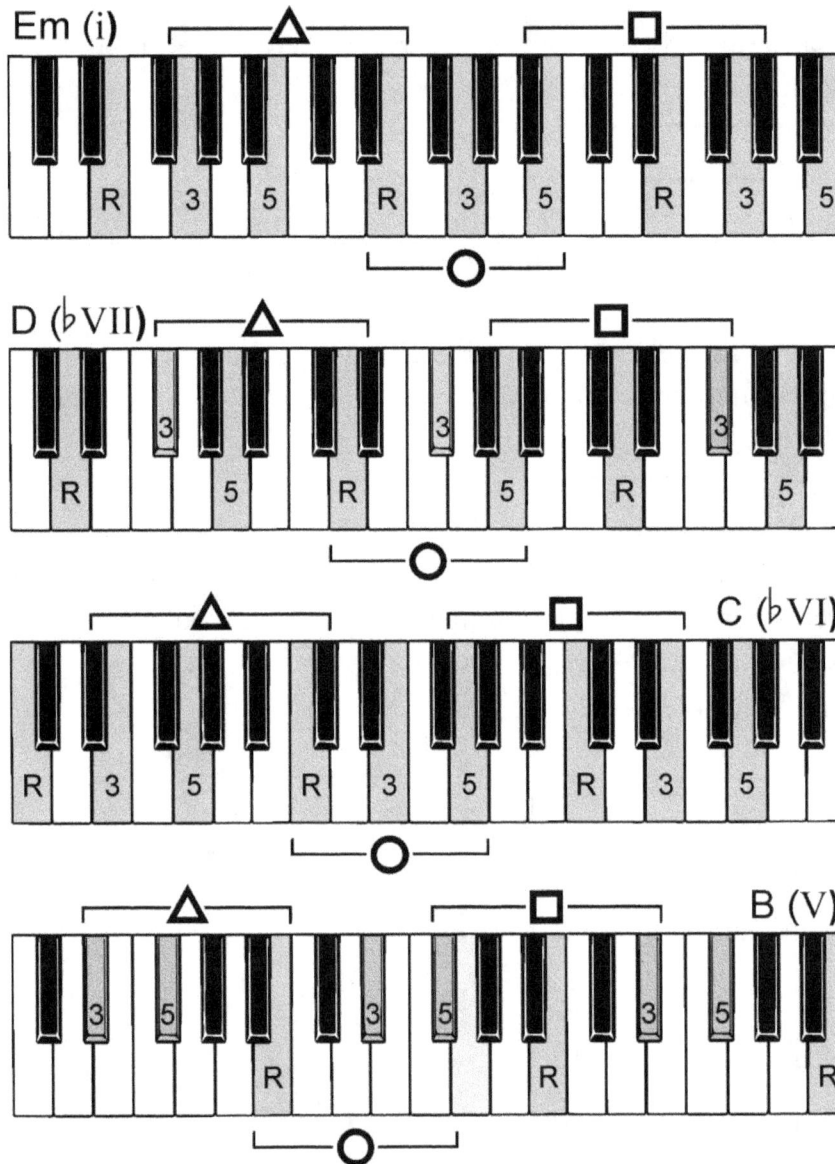

Em (i)

D (♭VII)

C (♭VI)

B (V)

Four-chord-tone keyboard textures

In Spanish Sketches (the module performance), there are usually four chord tones in use – the root, the fifth, the octave (next root note up) and the third, here called the tenth because it's above the octave, but the same note anyway.

These four notes get divided up between the two hands in various ways which can be shown in a table. The table on the right shows the right hand playing three notes and the left hand playing just the root. This is the first distribution as shown on the next page.

Rehearse the i–♭VII–♭VI–V chord sequence with the chord tones divided up as shown on the next page

The chord tones used		Which hand plays them
10	R	
8	R	
5	R	
R	L	

①

10	R
8	R
5	R
R	L

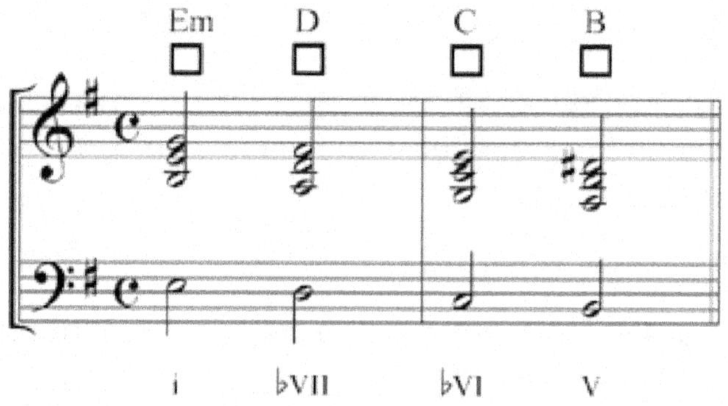

②

10	R
8	R
5	L
R	L

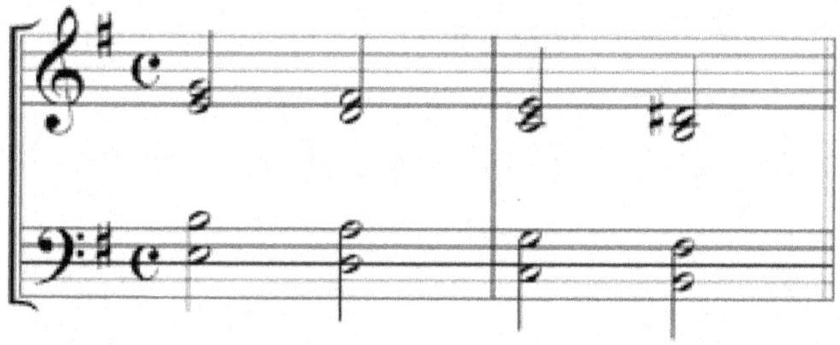

③

8	R
5	L
3	L
R	L

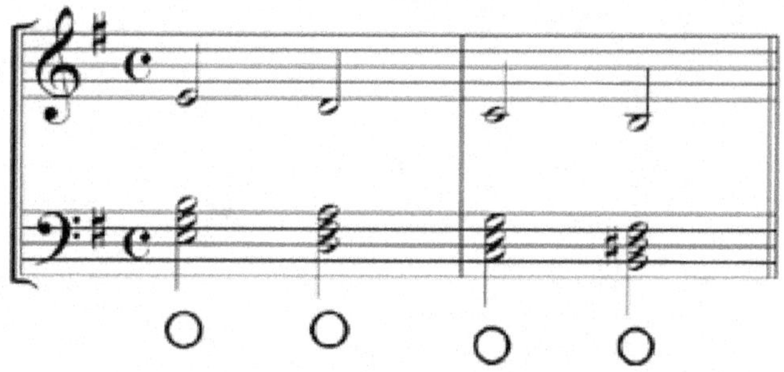

④

5	R
3	R
R	R
R	L

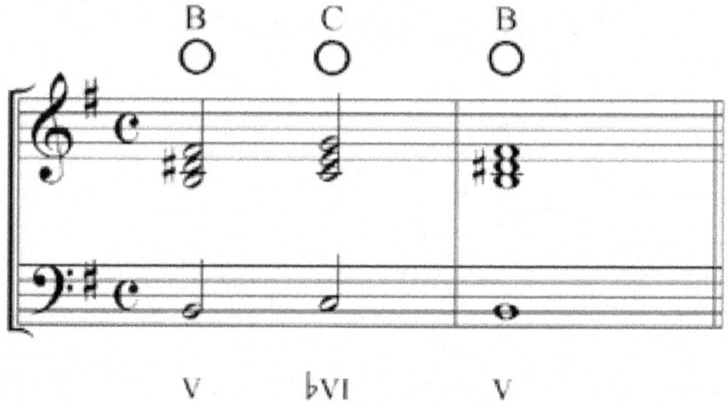

⑤

8	R
5	R
3	R
R	L

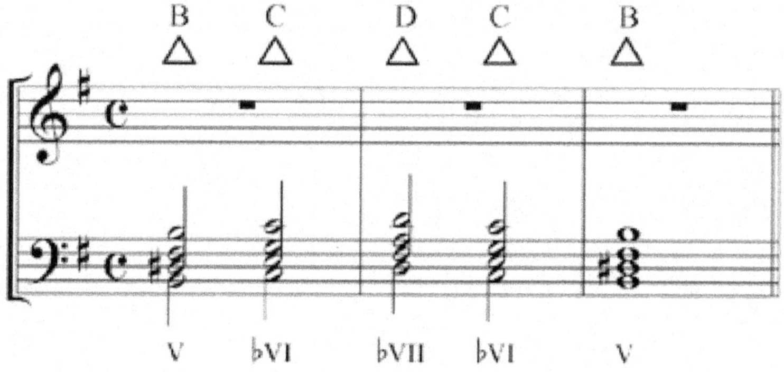

sup_spa_04

It's important to be able to play the same chord tones in several different ways. It teaches you what the chord tones really are, independent of which hand or finger plays them. Your time on the above exercise will be well spent.

Building up the Spanish Sketches performance

This module's performance consists of segments you can play and join together in any number of different ways.

Get to know the meter (rhythm) of the Sketches – a slow three-four – with this preparatory exercise, using the first division of the chords tones from the table above. Use the 'official' fingering (1, 3, 5) for the right hand second inversion chords.

(Note: The audio clip goes on to play the next development. You could use the opportunity to 'play it by ear'.)

sup_spa_05

In this rhythm, introduce the main melody in the left hand.

sup_spa_06

The melody starts half way through a bar. Count yourself in: "(One, two) and three and…".

The slash-and-dot symbol in the MS means 'play one bar exactly like the previous bar'. It's good to read musical shorthand like this – it gets you away from relying on 'the dots' (written-out music).

Developing the rhythm

Next, we develop the rhythm, playing chords in the off-beat quaver 'slots'. The 'off-beat slots' are the non-number 'and' (&) slots. Here's a simple riff to practice playing on the off beat in the right hand.

sup_spa_07

Make a note of the rhythm and tap it on your desktop.

Now use that right hand with the original left hand melody. An introduction is included to build up some momentum.

sup_spa_08

Here's a tapping exercise for the two patterns involved, plus a possible way of splitting up and 'waggling' the right hand chords.

sup_spa_09   sup_spa_10

The second division of chord tones

Our next theme uses the second division of the chord tones from the main table – two in the right hand, two in the left. Prepare the segment, then play the following music from the MS and/or the audio clip.

sup_spa_11

You can hear how the segments you've learnt so far can be 'stitched together' in the Spanish Sketches audio at the start of the module.

Off-beat quavers in the left hand

This segment uses the third division of the chord tones between the hands (Three right, one left - see the table).

Playing off-beat quaver chords in the left hand as well as the bass notes is quite a trick to master. Here is a build-up to the full pattern, with audio clips at a comfortable practice speed.

1. The tune is in the right hand. The left hand plays a root position chord (circle symbol) on beat 2.

sup_spa_12

2. The left hand chord splits into the bass note and the other two chord tones.

147

sup_spa_13

3. Now practice chords on the off-beat quavers (the 'ands'/&).

sup_spa_14

4. Then divide the left hand chord into bass note and chord tones as before. The left hand may need quite a lot of solo practice.

sup_spa_15

If you don't get the full pattern first time round, use one of the build-up versions in your performance for the time being – but keep pushing yourself. Don't get so hypnotised by the written-out notes that you can't use the counting and TLR analysis – they really are the only way forward for a lot of learners.

Here is an audio/MIDI file for the whole of this part rhythmic build-up.

sup_spa_16

Right hand off the-beat chords

This pattern might sound familiar.

sup_spa_17

Your chord work will sound a lot more interesting if you 'riffle' the chords, as if you were strumming a guitar. You can hear this effect on some of the right hand chords in the performance audio clip.

Here's another 'typical' segment which is divided three right, one left.

sup_spa_18

This pattern uses the last 'division of the chord tones' in the table, with first inversions (triangle symbol) in the right hand and just the root in the left.

It's even in a different meter (time signature), but it fits in quite naturally. A possible continuation is shown. (This would also be a good place to go into your improvisation.) The fermata sign tells you can wait as long as you like before going on – a good idea when you're changing meter again.

Improvising a solo

At some stage, you are going to want to try improvising a melody, and the B and C major chords are a good place to do this. The sample audio which follows has a lazy three-four

149

rhythm, but you can drop the rhythm all together if you like. Aim for chord tones on the main beat in the right hand over a free left hand.

Listen to some Spanish flamenco guitar music on YouTube for inspiration. Search Paco Pena (ex. Tientos De La Bahía), Paco De Lucia, and 'flamenco guitar'.

(Both the harmony and rhythm of flamenco music are very complex, as you'll soon discover. *Spanish Sketches* is a simplified version, to help you get carried away by the music.)

The improvised melody section of the module audio is towards the middle of the clip. It's the only part which doesn't have written-out music.

> sup_spa_01

Creating your own performance

The *Spanish Sketches* performance segments you have learnt in this module can easily be varied and put together in a different order to make a performance all your own.

Remember that, in this module particularly, you are not just looking for ways to be good, or right, but for ways to enjoy your own playing. The chord changes in the Spanish Sketches are very evocative and offer a good opportunity to be carried away by even your own playing.

MODES MASTER CHORD DIAGRAMS

The following tables present the useful chords in the Ionian, Mixolydian, Aeolian and Dorian modes in keys up to four sharps, four flats.

The chords are arranged with the tonic (home chord) in the middle column, a potentially more creative way of thinking about the chords in the modal families than thinking of the tonic (home chord) as always being the lowest chord.

The classical key signatures which produce the mode tones for the given tonic are shown in the left-most column. These are unlikely to be used in written modal music – generally, the 'proper' classical key signature will be used but accidentals in the MS will reveal the modal nature of the music.

The diminished triad has been omitted from these tables, leaving families of six chords. The diminished triad is unstable and serves mainly to furnish the top three notes of a dominant seventh chord. The naturally occurring dominant sevenths in the modes are:

Ionian: V7   Mixolydian: I7   Aeolian: ♭VII7   Dorian: IV7

These seventh chords will have a strong tendency to cadence out of the mode and into the classical tonic chord of the modal family – IV in the Mixolydian, ♭III in the Aeolian and ♭VII in the Dorian.

These tables can easily be used to structure keyboard compositions. As a starting point, start on the tonic chord and stray up and down (i.e. right and left along the rows). Try out some mediant substitution in your meanderings by dropping the left hand bass note a scale third or taking the right hand triad up a third (essentially, adding the seventh chord tone).

Remember that the modern musical ear tends to want to pull the music out of the mode and back into the classical major (Ionian mode) or minor, so make a point of finishing back on your modal tonic (home) chord, preserving the modal harmonic tension.

IONIAN MODE

Mode as scale

C IONIAN   (White keys from C to C = C major scale. Key signature as per tonic.)   Regular major scale

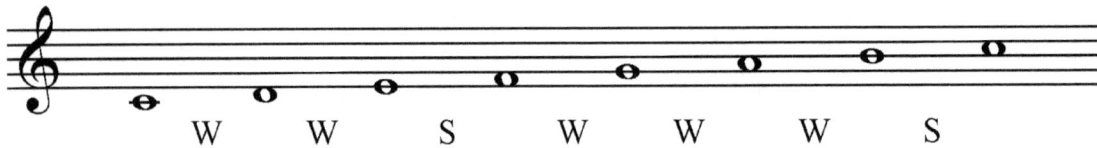

W   W   S   S   W   W   W   S

Chord families

KEY SIG	CHORD	Sub-dominant	Dominant	Sub-mediant	TONIC	Super-tonic	Mediant	Sub-dominant
		IV	V	vi	I	ii	iii	IV
C		F	G	Am	C	Dm	Em	F
G		C	D	Em	G	Am	Bm	C
D		G	A	Bm	D	Em	F♯m	G
A		D	E	F♯m	A	Bm	C♯m	D
E		A	B	C♯m	E	F♯m	G♯m	A
C		F	G	Am	C	Dm	Em	F
F		B♭	C	Dm	F	Gm	Am	B♭
B♭		E♭	F	Gm	B♭	Cm	Dm	E♭
E♭		A♭	B♭	Cm	E♭	Fm	Gm	A♭
A♭		D♭	E♭	Fm	A♭	B♭m	Cm	D♭

MIXOLYDIAN MODE

Mode as scale

C MIXOLYDIAN   (White keys G to G = F major scale from C to C. Key signature a perfect fourth up.)   Dominant scale

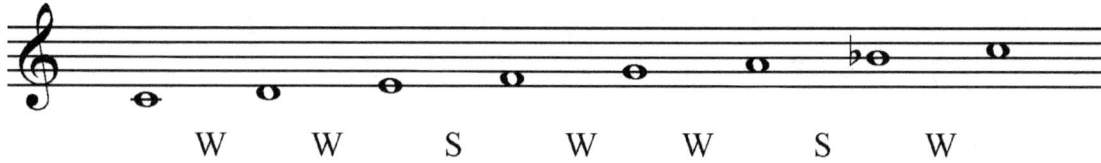

W   W   S   W   W   S   W

Chord families

KEY SIG	CHORD	Dominant	Sub-mediant	Leading note	TONIC	Super-tonic	Sub-dominant	Dominant
		v	vi	♭VII	I	ii	IV	v
F		Gm	Am	B♭	C	Dm	F	Gm
C		Dm	Em	F	G	Am	C	Dm
G		Am	Bm	C	D	Em	G	Am
D		Em	F♯m	G	A	Bm	D	Em
A		Bm	C♯m	D	E	F♯m	A	Bm
C		Gm	Am	B♭	C	Dm	F	Gm
B♭		Cm	Dm	E♭	F	Gm	B♭	Cm
E♭		Fm	Gm	A♭	B♭	Cm	E♭	Fm
A♭		B♭m	Cm	D♭	E♭	Fm	A♭	B♭m
D♭		E♭m	Fm	G♭	A♭	B♭m	D♭	E♭m

AEOLIAN MODE

Mode as scale

C AEOLIAN (White keys A to A = E♭ major scale from C to C. Key signature a minor third up.) 'Natural minor' scale

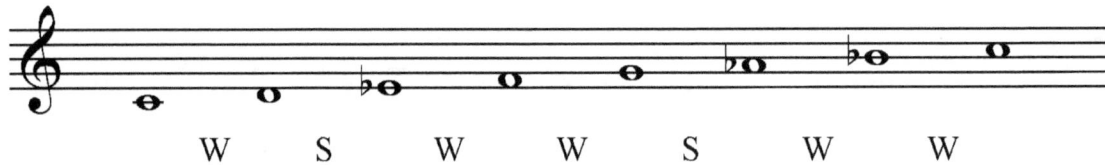

W   S   W   W   S   W   W

Chord families

KEY SIG	CHORD	Dominant	Sub-mediant	Leading note	TONIC	Mediant	Sub-dominant	Dominant
		v	♭VI	♭VII	i	♭III	iv	v
E♭		Gm	A♭	B♭	Cm	E♭	Fm	Gm
B♭		Dm	E♭	F	Gm	B♭	Cm	Dm
F		Am	B♭	C	Dm	F	Gm	Am
C		Dm	F	G	Am	C	Dm	Dm
G		Bm	C	D	Em	G	Am	Bm
E♭		Gm	A♭	B♭	Cm	E♭	Fm	Gm
A♭		Cm	Dm	E♭	Fm	A♭	B♭m	Cm
D♭		Fm	Gm	A♭	B♭m	D♭	E♭m	Fm
G♭		B♭m	Cm	D♭	E♭m	G♭	A♭m	B♭m
C♭		E♭m	Fm	G♭	A♭m	C♭	D♭m	E♭m

154

DORIAN MODE

Mode as scale

C DORIAN (White keys D to D = B♭ major scale from C to C. Key signature a whole tone below.) Minor, major sixth

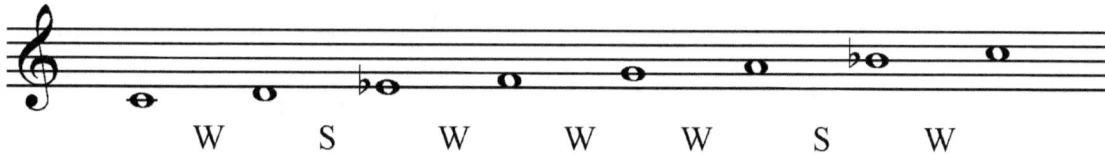

W S W W W S W

Chord families

KEY SIG	CHORD	Sub-dominant	Dominant	Leading note	TONIC	Super-tonic	Mediant	Sub-dominant
		IV	v	♭VII	i	ii	♭III	IV
B♭		F	Gm	B♭	Cm	Dm	E♭	F
F		C	Dm	F	Gm	Am	B♭	C
C		G	Am	C	Dm	Em	F	G
G		D	Dm	G	Am	Bm	C	D
B♭		A	Bm	D	Em	F#m	G	A
B♭		F	Gm	B♭	Cm	Dm	E♭	F
E♭		B♭	Cm	E♭	Fm	Gm	A♭	B♭
A♭		E♭	Fm	A♭	B♭m	Cm	D♭	E♭
D♭		A♭	B♭m	D♭	E♭m	Fm	G♭	A♭
G♭		D♭	E♭m	G♭	A♭m	B♭m	C♭	D♭

MUSICARTA MODES WORKBOOK – SUPPLEMENT THREE

MEPS AS MODES

Most of the piano solos in the Musicarta Easy Piano Style (MEPS) workbook have modal chord sequences. You can listen to all the solos on the Mister Musicarta YouTube Musicarta Easy Piano Style playlist.

Here are short descriptions of the pieces.

The purpose of this page is twofold – firstly, to offer more listening which is 'certified 100% modal' and thereby stimulate the readers interest in modes, and secondly to walk the reader through the process of establishing whether a chord sequence is in fact modal.

First Pair of Chords

The First Pair of Chords performance uses chords C and D minor, with C as the tonic. The chords are therefore I and ii and the piece is in the simple major, and doesn't display modal harmony.

Second Pair of Chords

The Second Pair of Chords study also uses a pair of chords a whole tone apart (E minor and D), but with the upper, minor chord the tonic. The chords are therefore a i–♭VII pair, and the piece is therefore modal in its harmony. Both the Aeolian and Dorian modes have i–♭VII pairs, but the piece doesn't have a subdominant (iv in the Aeolian, IV in the Dorian) so we are unable to say which mode definitively. The Aeolian mode is the more common minor mode however, so we would default to Aeolian for this piece.

One Fourth and a Pair

Here is the chord sequence for the One Fourth and a Pair study – *The Vigil.*

1

Am	Em	Am	Em	Am	Em	D	Em

33   *(repeats)*

D	Em	D	D	Em	Em	

The piece starts with an A minor chord but ends on E minor, and listening to the piece should convince you that E minor is the home chord or tonic, and therefore i. Counting round our musical alphabet, we find we have a iv chord (A minor) and a ♭VII chord (D major). The piece is therefore in the Aeolian mode – E Aeolian.

Three Fourths and a Pair

Here is the chord sequence for Three Fourths and a Pair.

Am	Em	F	C	Dm	Am	G	Am

The study starts and ends on A minor and a listen should convince you that this is indeed the home chord. Counting from A = i, we find our chord sequence is:

| i | v | ♭VI | ♭III | iv | i | ♭VII | i |

The minor subdominant iv chord confirms that the study is in A Aeolian.

Three Fourths – E minor Variations

The next study transposes the same chord sequence into E minor.

Em	Bm	C	G	Am	Em	D	Em

As an exercise, count off the chords to make sure you see how it is the same sequence.

| i | v | ♭VI | ♭III | iv | i | ♭VII | i |

Tanza

Here is the Tanza chord sequence.

'A' strain

Am	G	Am	G	Am	G	F :G	Am	F :G	Am

'B' strain

Am:Em	F :C	Dm:Am	G :Am	Am:Em	F :C	Dm:Am	G	G	Am	Am

Look at the roots of the first line – A, G and F, all a whole tone apart, the highest of which is a minor chord. Only A minor, G and F chords on the all-white keys match that profile, so the first line is definitely in A Aeolian. The second line is the chord sequence from 'Three Fourths and a Pair', above, so the whole piece is in A Aeolian without a doubt.

Afternoon

Afternoon is pure diatonic major – 'diatonic' meaning, without any chromatic alterations to the key chords (no accidentals, in practical terms). It therefore uses only the i, ii, iii, IV, V and vi Ionian (pure major) chords. Listen to it for comparison with the modal tonalities you have been hearing.

Ever True

Here is the *Ever True* chord sequence.

1, 17, 33 ('A strain')

Am	Am	G	G	Am	Am	G	G

9, 25 ('B strain')

F	F	G	G	F	F	G	G

41 (ending – ladders)

Am	Am	Am	Am

Not much doubt that the piece is in A minor. A minor therefore = i, and the G and F chords will be ♭VII and ♭VI respectively – the i–♭VII–♭VI group of chords from the Aeolian One module.

Fanfare   V

Here is the chord sequence of *Fanfare*.

1, 9   *(repeats)*

Am	F :C	G :Am	F :C	G :Am	F :C	G	G

Extended ladder ending

C	C	C	C

The A minor chord could have a claim to be the tonic of an A Aeolian piece here, but the fanfare eventually resolves to the major C chord, so the piece is in C major with the A minor emphasis used for colour.

An Unsettling Notion

These two lines of the *Unsettling Notion* chord sequence include all the chords used in the piece.

1

Am	G :D	Am :D	Am :D	Am	G :D	Am :D	Am :D

9   *(repeats)*

C	G :D	Am :D	Am :D	C	G :D	Am :D	Am :D

As the piece ends with four bars of A minor, we work on the assumption that that is the home chord/tonic – i. The other chords therefore line up ♭VII (G), IV (D) and ♭III (C). The i–♭III–IV–♭VII group of chords is a typical Dorian selection. Recall that the Dorian subdominant ('Four') chord is major (IV), while the Aeolian 'Four' is minor – iv.

MEPS Diary 29-06-13 (*A Dilemma*)

Here is the chord MEPS Diary 29-06-13 chord sequence.

1

Am	Am	F :G	Am	Am	Am	F :G	Am

9

F :G	C :F	Dm7:G	C	F :G	Am :F	Dm7:G	

16

Am	Am	F :G	Am	Am	Am	F :G	Am

The first line of this chord sequence should strike you forcible as an A Aeolian i–♭VII–♭VI group of chords. The only shadow of doubt is raised by the Dm7 chord – which is, of course, the F chord with the dropped submediant D bass, producing D minor 7.

MEPS Diary 12-11-13 – Riff in Sixths

Here is the riff chord sequence.

Am	G	Am	G	C	B♭	Am	G

The Am–G pair of chords should immediately have you thinking "i-♭VII modal minor", but then you come up against the B♭ chord. If A minor is the tonic, B♭ is ♭II – a major chord built on a root just one semitone higher. Examining your knowledge of the chords built on and out of the C major scale tones – which we know will always be 'modal' - we find the E minor–F major pair fits the pattern. The riff could therefore conceivably be in the Locrian mode (E to E white keys and chords), but for the fact that the F natural will make the Locrian 'flat seven' chord <u>minor</u> – D minor in E Locrian. The flat seven chord here, however, is major (G - ♭VII). The chord sequence is therefore not modal.

Naomi - Fantasie

Naomi – Fantasie is the showcase of the Musicarta Easy Piano Style album. Here is its chord sequence.

'A' strain (1, 9, 53, 61)   (repeats)

Am	Em	Am	Em	Am	Em	D	Em

(extended ending – 17, 69)

D	D	Em	Em

'B' strain (21, 45)

Am: ~6	Am:~6	Em	Em	Am: ~6	Am:~6	Em	Em

'C' strain (29, 37)   (repeats)

Am	Am	G	G	D	D	Em	Em

Repeated end-of-strain E minor chords give the key at least away – as E minor (= i). The absence of any B major chords (V, 'Five' – the principle cadencing chord of the classical minor key) suggest a modal tonality, and the D major chord before every tonic (♭VII acting as the cadencing chord) confirm it.

Other chords appearing are A minor (= iv) and G major (= ♭III). We do not need any more chords to establish the key as E Aeolian modal. Even the sixth added to the A minor chord in the B strain (an F sharp) stays in key.